Praise for Chris McGoff and *The PRIMES*...

"The PRIMES is a user's guide for taking on challenging transformations.... I have seen firsthand how the fundamental truths outlined in The PRIMES can make the impossible possible. Read The PRIMES if you would like to look at difficult and complicated challenges through a different lens."

Major General Craig Bambrough
(US Army, retired)

"Chris McGoff has scoured the world for the best back-of-the-napkin diagrams—those rough-penciled graphic maps to human and group relationships that smack you between the eyes and make you shout, 'Yes! That explains it!!' He's tested these "PRIMES" in the crucible of real-life consulting—and has the stories to prove it. Only Chris could have married vision and practice in this way, and given us such a readable guide to why life works."

Rushworth M. Kidder
President and Founder, Institute for Global Ethics
Author of *How Good People Make Tough Choices*
and *Moral Courage*

"Michael Doyle was an early innovator in the development and use of the thinking tools contained in Chris McGoff's work, The PRIMES. The book is a tribute to the wonderful creativity that Michael and Chris shared in their work together."

Juli Betwee
Managing Partner, Pivot Point Partners

"In the final analysis, everything we try to accomplish in business, government, and in our community involves human beings. As I navigate the challenging task of encouraging collaboration among the human beings of the world, Chris's generous compilation of this set of universal truths in the form of The PRIMES has proven invaluable time and again to me."

Tim Hurlebaus
Vice President, Consulting Services CGI, Europe and Asia

"Leaders ... in the throes of changing, or, more important, transforming an organization ... are involved in some of the most challenging events of their lives. So much so, that [they] can be measured by the scars of

*the experience versus the successes. After reading **The PRIMES**, my approach toward those monumental efforts will be much different. This book has clearly outlined how an organization can succeed based upon the experience of others without suffering the pains of past efforts.... [If I were] given another chance at transforming an organization, Chris would be with me in spirit through the tattered pages that I would read and re-read as my roadmap! Anyone who has ever solved a problem on a napkin will love this book; it is how many problems are solved."*

Mo McGowan
Former Assistant Administrator for Security Operations,
Transportation Security Administration
US Department of Homeland Security

"What do the United Nations, the US Department of Defense, the International Finance Corporation, and the World Bank have in common? When they ran into problems, they called Chris McGoff. Why? Solutions. They needed them. Chris showed them how to find them. Read his book, and he'll do the same for you."

Larry Danner
Head of School, Washington Christian Academy
Educational Consultant

"In this deceptively simple set of guiding principles, Chris combines acute power of observation, profound understanding of and empathy for human behavior, clarity of thinking, creativity, and, perhaps most important, courage. Spend some quiet time in self-reflection on each PRIME to identify those areas where you can grow as a person and as a leader."

Chris Smith
Chief Operating Officer
US Green Building Council

*"Determined to bring the best-quality health care to the poor in Kenya, I floundered, wondering where to start. The best thing that happened to me at that critical time was having the benefit of a few days of Chris's time. We did not know then that the new venture we called 'LiveWell Health Clinics' was designed and formulated around **The PRIMES**. Chris encouraged us to 'envision boldly,' build in integrity and trust as core values, and declare with date-certain outcomes the transformation we were making. He freely shared his wisdom and helped us see with greater clarity the needs of our people, by talking to hundreds of*

*potential customers. This approach is by far the best foundation we could have laid for our company. I am so pleased that Chris has now published all this wisdom in this book. I have tried and tested the wisdom of **The PRIMES**, with phenomenal results, and highly recommend it for one and all!"*

Liza Kimbo
CEO, LiveWell Clinics, Kenya

*"Chris McGoff has distilled the primary rules of the road for outstanding consulting work, in collaboration with a pioneer in facilitation, Michael Doyle. **The PRIMES** are clear, visually iconized, and pure gold as guides to organization transformation. They're the keystone 'apps' for change."*

David Sibbet
The Grove Consultants International

*"I found Chris's advice in **The PRIMES** to be profound, easy to grasp, and easy to share with my team. The illustrations are clever and memorable. Don't let the simplicity of the presentation fool you; **The PRIMES** is one of the most useful and powerful books I've ever read."*

Lori Bacon
President & Owner, Swimco, Inc.

*"Not only is my team more engaged, empowered, and energized than before, I am at ease knowing that I don't always have to have all the answers or ideas in order to be an effective leader. **The PRIMES** provides simple and easy to remember concepts that illustrate leadership and organizational savvy. From the 'CORE PRIME' to 'IN-ON,' each PRIME provides both the insight and the tool to successfully navigate through uncertain times."*

Leslie A. Firtell, Esq.
President & CEO
Tower Legal Solutions

THE
PRIMES

THE

PRIMES

HOW ANY GROUP CAN
SOLVE ANY PROBLEM

CHRIS McGOFF

WILEY

John Wiley & Sons, Inc.

Published by John Wiley & Sons, Inc., Hoboken, New Jersey.
Published simultaneously in Canada.

For general information on our other products and services or for technical support, please contact our Customer Care Department within the United States at (800) 762-2974, outside the United States at (317) 572-3993 or fax (317) 572-4002.

Wiley publishes in a variety of print and electronic formats and by print-on-demand. Some material included with standard print versions of this book may not be included in e-books or in print-on-demand. If this book refers to media such as a CD or DVD that is not included in the version you purchased, you may download this material at http://booksupport.wiley.com. For more information about Wiley products, visit www.wiley.com.

Library of Congress Cataloging-in-Publication Data:

McGoff, Chris, 1957-
  The primes : how any group can solve any problem / Chris McGoff.
    p. cm.
  ISBN 978-1-118-17327-5 (pbk)
  ISBN 978-1-118-22680-3 (ebk)
  ISBN 978-1-118-24004-5 (ebk)
  ISBN 978-1-118-26465-2 (ebk)
  1. Group problem solving. I. Title.
  HD30.29.M39 2013
  658.4′036–dc23

                                        2011050887

Printed in the United States of America

10 9 8 7 6 5 4 3 2 1

To Michael,
for living large and being generous.

To Claire,
for encouraging me to live unreasonably.

To designers of the future everywhere,
for giving me hope and purpose.

ACKNOWLEDGMENTS

This book exists because of my shared experiences and relationships with a group of gifted and generous people. In 1987, I was asked by IBM to investigate the intersection of group performance with network technology. This was a unique moment in time. We brought together business minds, social and behavioral scientists, and technologists. This effort benefited from the significant contributions and insights of IBM leaders, including Ray Duel, Ron Dougherty, Ann Hunt, and Ron Grohowski. Joining the effort was Jay Nunamaker and his team at the University of Arizona; Paul Gray, Claremont; Larry Phillips, London School of Economics; Jerry Wagner, University of Nebraska; Paul Saffo, Discern; and Robert Johansen, Institute for the Future, Palo Alto, CA. The project led to the development and release of IBM's Teamfocus groupware application.

I also acknowledge the companies that invited us into their businesses to experiment and apply the technologies in real business environments, including Procter and Gamble, J. P. Morgan, American Airlines, the US Coast Guard, General Motors, DuPont, Boeing, The Women's Presidents Organization, and The World Bank. I am forever grateful for your curiosity, patience, and trust. I offer special acknowledgment to Col. Robert Glitz, Gen. Donald Shepperd, and Gen. William Navas for giving us an opportunity to consolidate our insights in 1991; launch an independent company, which became Touchstone Consulting; and support the transformation of the US National Guard. You demanded better of us than we initially thought possible.

James Wolfensohn, Christine Wallich, and Dennis Whittle provided an opportunity to stress test our emerging insights, distinctions, and methods regarding group performance in a realm of extreme stakeholder complexity. The transformation of the World Bank involved people from all over the world with different backgrounds, needs, traditions, cultures, and customs. This seven-year project and its related projects at the United Nations, International Monetary Fund, and Asian Development Bank catalyzed our learning and demonstrated the consistency of group dynamics throughout the world. These experiences provided the mandate to strip the PRIMES to their essence and render each of them as simple and universally accessible images.

These projects, and many more like them, provided the opening for me to work side by side with people passionate about group performance, including Michael Doyle, Juli Betwee, Kai Dozier, Regina Perkins, Steve Lynott, David Sibbet, Paul Safo, Deirdre Crowley, Lenny Lynn, Lance Dublin, and the folks at Touchstone Consulting, Inc., to name a few.

This book also consolidates ideas from many contemporary sources, including the works of Russ Akoff, Fernando Flores, Werner Erhard, John Austin, John Searle, Peter Senge, Daniel Kim, Peter Keen, Michael Gerber, and Rush Kidder.

Scott Williams and Sarah Cheffy, of MAGA Design, helped put the overall concept of this book together. Tom Taylor, Marybeth Fraser, Dana Theus, Patrick Kane, Cristin Datch, Ellen Burns, Dennis Kane, Tom Wade, Marie France, John Miller, and the folks at Morgan James Publishing made the first edition possible. This second edition exists because of contributions by Christian Ulstrup, Shaye Swanson, Paige Douglass, Jonathan Spector, and the folks at John Wiley & Sons, Inc., including Richard Narramore, Susan Moran, Peter Knox, and Lydia Dimitriadis.

I also acknowledge the people of The Clearing, Inc. You are the agents of change our world is calling for. I am fascinated by how you apply the PRIMES every day in the context of some of the most complex problems on the planet. Your courage, intentionality, and persistence in helping our government and global corporations solve wicked, high stakes problems inspire me. You are creating a better world, one leader at a time.

In the same way, I am grateful for my children's interest in the PRIMES. Ryan, Brock, Carli, James, Casey, and Erin—know that our conversations about the PRIMES and how you see them occurring in your world have affected the contents of this book. "Hey dad, I used a PRIME today!" is always followed by a discussion in which I learn something.

Finally, the PRIMES belong to the collective human experience. Others have expressed many of the ideas shared in these pages. I've included endnotes to reference sources that I've found uniquely and significantly valuable. I apologize to all whom a more diligent scholar would have cited. Any value I add is in assembling, ordering, and naming these universal phenomena—the PRIMES.

We're here to put a dent in the universe. Otherwise why else even be here?

ॐ Steve Jobs

A NOTE TO THE READER

There is no wrong way to read *The PRIMES*. You can read it cover to cover, scan the contents and explore whatever PRIME jumps off the page, or randomly open the book to any section and be surprised.

My colleagues and I never experienced the PRIMES in their entirety and neatly organized. Each PRIME occurred to us "just in time" and in no apparent order. You need not set your sights on mastering all 46 PRIMES straight out of the gate. Simply master the few you need right now. You will know which ones they are. Keep the book handy. When you are ready, the next relevant PRIME will jump off the page.

My hope is that you experience the PRIMES as Dr. Rushworth Kidder, founder of the Institute for Global Ethics, did when he said,

> *That explains it. Reading* The PRIMES *was a blinding shock of the obvious!*

May the PRIMES help you to live huge, be intentional, and "persist variously"!

The beginning of wisdom is the correct naming of things.

ॐ Confucius

CONTENTS

INTRODUCTION xxv

PART I: UNIVERSAL PATTERNS OF LEADING IN UNCERTAIN TIMES I

How do some people, organizations, and coalitions thrive in uncertain times? What enables them to appear so certain and take decisive action amid ambiguity about the future?

CHAPTER I – **BEING CLEAR ON WHAT'S REALLY IMPORTANT** 3

How did you decide how you spent your time yesterday? What criteria are you using to allocate your time tomorrow?

LEADING 5

Does being called a "leader" mean you are "leading"? What does "leading" mean?

IN–ON 9

Are you seduced by working "in" the business at the expense of "on" it?

CHANGE versus TRANSFORMATION 13

Are you fixing or creating?

CHAPTER 2 – **BEING INTENTIONAL AND GOING FIRST** 18

What are you committed to making happen and by when? What does "committed" mean? What does your commitment mean to others?

INTEGRITY 21

Does your "yes" really mean "yes"?

TRUST THE UNIVERSE 25
Is your vision limited to what you've already seen?

DECLARATION.. 29
Are you willing to live unreasonably?

CHAPTER 3 – **ENROLLING OTHERS**.................................... 32
Can you call people, from disenfranchisement and mere compliance, to their highest level of commitment?

DYNAMIC INCOMPLETENESS 35
Can you create a vision that is compelling because of what it says and at the same time inviting—for what it leaves yet to be said?

ENNOBLEMENT 39
Does your vision elevate people in degree and excellence and respect and inspire them to act boldly?

POWER... 45
Do you know how to turn strangers, competitors, cautious allies, and suspicious stakeholders into powerful, outcome-driven coalitions?

PART 2: **UNIVERSAL PATTERNS OF POWERFUL ALLIANCES** 47
How do you generate unprecedented power within the group? Is this question all that important to you?

CHAPTER 4 – **GAINING SHARED PERSPECTIVE**....................... 49
Everyone claims to value diversity. Can maintaining diverse perspectives ever be a bad thing?

BLIND MEN AND THE ELEPHANT 51
How do you help people to see the "whole thing"?

LEVELS OF PERSPECTIVE 55

How do you help people to see the same "whole thing"?

S-CURVES 59

How do you lead people to a shared sense of now?

CHAPTER 5 – **ESTABLISHING SHARED INTENT** 62

How do you lead the group to be intentional?

CORE PRIME 65

How do you help the group to focus on the right things and feel urgent about acting?

PARITY 73

What is the right ratio of analyzing versus imagining?

STAKE 77

How do you get the group "all in"?

CHAPTER 6 – **TAKING COORDINATED ACTION** 80

How do you get the group to do everything persistently about a few critical things versus doing a few things about everything?

COHESION 83

Cohesion is an unnatural state for a group. How good are you at establishing and sustaining it?

REDPOINT 85

A good question to ask is, "What is important to do?" A better question is, "Of all the important things we could do, what are the fewest, most important?"

MUDA 93

Can you distinguish "non-value-added activity"? How much of your group's resources is it consuming?

PART 3: **UNIVERSAL PATTERNS OF OUTSTANDING GROUP PERFORMANCE**.......96
What do high-performance groups know and do that low-performance groups do not?

CHAPTER 7 – **MAKING DECISIONS** 98
What does the word "decision" actually mean? How are decisions made?

LEADERSHIP SPECTRUM 101
Are you the kind of leader who likes to facilitate consensus? The right answer is, "That depends."

CONSENSUS 105
Are you still using the traditional definition of consensus? Are you aware of how destructive the traditional definition is?

OPEN–CLOSE–DECIDE 109
How do groups actually make decisions?

CHAPTER 8 – **BUILDING AN INTENTIONAL CULTURE** 113
Quick—what does "culture" mean? There are consequences to using more than seven words to define culture.

CULTURE...115
Culture happens. You shape it or it shapes you. How good are you at shaping a culture?

CONGRUENCE 119
What is the dark side of a stated culture?

FEEDBACK AS CARING 123
How good are you at giving it? How good are you at getting it? Why does it matter?

CHAPTER 9 – **SOCIAL CONTRACTING AND ACCOUNTABILITY WITHIN THE GROUP** 126

How do peers give each other commands?

REQUEST 129
Why saying "no" protects your saying "yes."

TRUST 133
We all say how important trust is. What is trust? How do you generate it and how do you destroy it?

BREACH 137
What do you do when your "yes" turns out to be a "no"?

CHAPTER 10 – **SAYING AND NOT SAYING; LISTENING AND NOT LISTENING** 140

How do high-performance groups sound?

PERIMETER 143
How small a fence have you built around what can and cannot be said?

FACTS, STORIES, AND BELIEFS 147
Can you distinguish facts from stories from beliefs? Do you use facts the way a drunk uses a lamp post—for support versus illumination?

GOSSIP 151
What is it? What makes it so destructive? How do you stop it?

PART 4: **UNIVERSAL PATTERNS OF GROUP FAILURE** 153
How good are you at anticipating, avoiding, and slaying the dragons that inevitably show up and threaten your group and the outcomes your group is standing for?

CHAPTER 11 – **OVERCOMING RESISTANCE** 155
Are you okay with favoring some people and ignoring others?

    LAGGARDS 157
    Do you know how to starve "possibility killers"?

    FRAGMENTATION 161
    How skilled are you at overcoming resistance from the powerful middle?

    SAME–DIFFERENT 165
    Everybody's special. Really?

CHAPTER 12 – **MANAGING INTRACTABLE DILEMMAS** 168
How do you end a never-ending argument?

    BIG HAT–LITTLE HAT 171
    What do you do when the needs of the many conflict with the needs of the few?

    RIGHT VERSUS RIGHT 175
    Resolving conflicts about right and wrong is child's play. How skilled are you at resolving matters of right versus right?

    RESOLUTION PRINCIPLES 179
    Right versus right arguments have been going on forever. What can we learn from our ancestors?

CHAPTER 13 – **AVOIDING TRIPPING HAZARDS**... 181

Tripping hazards are easier to avoid when you know where they are. When it comes to working in groups, can you see them coming?

CHASE–LOSE.. 183

Chase teamwork, leadership, morale, and culture and you will surely lose them all.

PROCESS–CONTENT.. 189

You can run the process. You can contribute to content. Pick one.

SHAPE SHIFTING.. 191

How to destroy your power in groups.

CHAPTER 14 – **REFUSING TO HIDE OUT**... 194

We all live our lives trying to avoid embarrassment. Can you recognize when you and your group are hiding out and playing safe?

VICTIM–LEADER... 197

What does "going victim" sound like?

COURT–LOCKER ROOM.. 199

Do you find planning to be a near-death experience?

CONFUSION 203

Why is confusion such a wonderful way of being?

PART 5: **UNIVERSAL PATTERNS OF THRIVING IN AMBIGUITY** 205
How do you stay healthy when the world is sick?

CHAPTER 15 – **AVOIDING BRIGHT AND SHINY OBJECTS AND SQUIRRELS**... 206
How do you manage distractions?

A CLEARING 209
How skilled are you at creating nothing?

ISSUES FORWARD 213
Looking behind and looking ahead are both important. What is the right ratio?

CHAPTER 16 – **TAKING GREAT CARE OF YOURSELF** 216
Can you give up coming from "something is wrong"?

COMMITMENT versus ATTACHMENT 219
Why saying "This project makes me so frustrated" is irrational.

BE 223
How good are you at cutting grass when you are cutting grass?

CONCLUSION: **NOW WHAT?**... 226
NOTES 228
INDEX OF THE PRIMES 237
ABOUT THE AUTHOR.. 239

INTRODUCTION

The world is resetting. It feels tipped now. Power, money, people, influence, and "coolness" are sliding around and pooling in new places. We are not sure where things are going to end up. Leading a business or any organization right now feels like shooting pool on the back of a small boat in high seas during a storm.

Eventually, the world will find its new stability. Eventually . . . maybe, but not in the foreseeable future. Managers and leaders are trying to guide their teams and organizations through these uncertain times. People are joining up in unprecedented alliances and coalitions to tackle problems that transcend any single organizational boundary.

At a minimum, the environment is imposing requirements for substantial change. Many of us are facing a mandate for wholesale transformation. *The PRIMES* is a gyroscope that you and your group can depend on to chart your best path, keep oriented, right the ship should the unexpected happen, and get to where you want to be, when you want to be there.

The PRIMES correctly names universal patterns of group behavior. The 46 PRIMES named in this book are not theories hatched in some lab; they're not new-fangled methodologies. They are phenomena as real as rocks and wind. They are an inextricable part of the human experience. PRIMES show up every time people join up in groups to solve problems, drive change, and transform systems. Like genes are to individuals, PRIMES are to groups. Whether you understand them or not, they determine a group's performance. Master the PRIMES and you can master leading groups. Master leading groups and you can tackle the toughest problems you face.

MASTERY OF "GROUP"—THE CRITICAL SKILL

In the face of the current world economic instability, uncertainty, and pace of change, some things are certain:

- **Joining Up**: Our capacity to form effective groups is essential to our survival. The unaligned individual is powerless against current forces of change and the challenges we are facing.

- **Teams**: Some of these groups will be traditional "teams" working at the unit and corporate level within a single organization. As in the past, the performance of these internal teams will make or break a company.

- **Loose Groups, Alliances, and Coalitions**: Many the problems we face cannot be solved within the confines of a single corporate or organizational entity. Problem-solving groups increasingly are coalitions of the willing and loose confederations of people drawn together from various loyalties, perspectives, and intentions.

Your ability to inspire people to join these groups, get aligned, generate sufficient power, and sustain that alignment and power until the problem is solved makes you a valuable resource and enables you to live huge and make a valuable and meaningful contribution to your community and the world at large.

Be warned. We as a people do not have a good track record of forming these groups and solving problems when stakeholder complexity is high. Most of these efforts fail outright. The rest usually go significantly over budget and finish late. Of the few projects that get completed, only one out of two meets minimal initial expectations.

The good news is that, outfitted with the PRIMES, you will beat these odds. You will recognize and decode the human behaviors that often appear on the surface as pure craziness when groups take on big problems. Once you understand the root causes to what's blocking progress, you can address them positively and with power. You'll be able to see things that others miss and anticipate things before they happen. Master the PRIMES and you can master leading and being part of highly effective groups and teams. Master the group, master your destiny. How many books make that claim?

THE ORIGIN OF THE PRIMES

Michael and I sat across the desk from Christina Wallich, the Director of Strategy for the World Bank. Between us were a dozen or so typed papers and diagrams. "So what do you think?" Christina asked.

This was the first time Michael Doyle and I had been inside the World Bank. Jumping out of a cab at the corner of 18th and I Streets in Washington, DC, I had noticed that the facade of the building looked like a gigantic spreadsheet, with block-long rows and columns of windows that expanded 13 stories into the sky. Seven thousand extraordinarily intelligent people work at the World Bank's headquarters, including the highest concentration of PhDs in the city and more than its share of renowned economists. Michael was one of my partners in a management consultancy we founded a few years earlier. He paid the cab driver, climbed out into the cool spring air, and shouted, "This is going to be so much fun!" I wasn't so sure.

Christina waited while Michael and I scanned the proposal on her desk. It described a design for the World Bank's soon-to-be-launched transformation process—one of the largest transformation initiatives ever attempted. The bank was 50 years old and under intense pressure to change its ways. People were actually in the streets chanting, "Fifty years is enough!" The stakes were high. Michael and I had been called in after the bank terminated its contract with one of the "Big Six" consulting firms. Our job was to review the plan for change.

I was a bit overwhelmed and was still trying to process all the material when Michael looked up from the documents, straight into Christina's eyes, and said, "It won't work." Christina hesitated before she said, "That's my sense as well. That's why you're here and the people who designed this are not. But what specifically do you see wrong with this process?" Michael took a piece of scrap paper and made two quick sketches. He labeled the first "The Rule of Problem/Solution Parity" and the second "Logic."

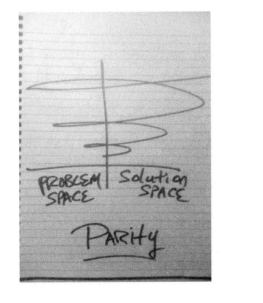

"First," Michael said, "this design won't work because it violates the 'Rule of Parity': People need approximately as much space to talk about the problem as they do the solution. This design creates far too little space for the bank's senior leaders to get sufficiently clear on the problem and too much space for solutions. The design also violates the natural logic of group planning and collaboration. Groups work best when they start with the 'As Is' and then move to the 'To Be,'" Michael explained. They need to start by thinking about the world and their outside environment and then consider what's going on in their organization. They need to start with their long-term plans and then move to their short-term plans. The current design had this all mixed up. "People will get lost," Michael said. "This process won't result in the outcomes you want and need."

Michael's little sketches, made in the heat of battle and just in time, enabled Christina to visualize and understand important principles that she hadn't been able to see previously. Through the lens of PARITY and LOGIC, she could see how the proposed design lacked balance and was illogical in its flow. If the plan were executed as it was designed, it would be sure to add to the chaotic environment that the bank's staff was already experiencing. We told Christina we would redesign the process by following the PARITY and LOGIC principles so that the organization would embrace it, from senior leadership down to frontline managers. We did, and it worked. The president of the World Bank Group at the time was James Wolfensohn. He and his 100-person leadership team enthusiastically plunged into our redesigned process, which resulted in building a clear strategy to transform the institution. Over the next several years, I worked with the bank to successfully implement the strategy.

The funny thing is, this is precisely the way all 46 PRIMES revealed themselves to Michael and me. They showed up "in the work" and usually when we were stuck—almost always just in time. And, it seems, usually on a scrap of paper or the back of a napkin.

I met Michael Doyle when I was working on developing groupware at IBM in the 1980s. I understood the technology and Michael understood groups. Over the 20 years of working together, we noticed that a select few of these little sketches kept showing up providing valuable insights. What intrigued us was how consistently the sketches provided value regardless of what part of the world we were in or what type of organization we were working with.

Michael and I began to catalogue these "blinding shocks of the obvious" insights. Our plan was to document them, organize them, and make them accessible to any and all who are leading or working in a team or group so that these people could be powerful and successful.

A few years ago, Michael suddenly died of a heart attack. At Michael's memorial service, change agents from all over the world gathered to pay their last respects to a master consultant, entrepreneur, and "Universe Denter" whose work had transformed organizations and communities large and small. We all considered him our mentor. I made a formal declaration to that group that I'd finish the job he and I had started. I'd assemble our most powerful sketches in a book that was short, visual, and could be easily absorbed in chunks—our on-the-job epiphanies, offered to any and all who were up to something big. I knew very little about publishing a book, but I trusted that everything I needed was out there somewhere and would come to my rescue. The world showed up and the book in your hands fulfills that promise.

Our deepest fear is not that we are inadequate. Our deepest fear is that we are powerful beyond measure. It is our light, not our darkness, that most frightens us. We ask ourselves, "Who am I to be brilliant, gorgeous, talented, fabulous?" Actually, who are you not to be? You are a child of God. Your playing small does not serve the world. There is nothing enlightened about shrinking so that other people won't feel insecure around you. We are all meant to shine, as children do. We were born to make manifest the glory of God that is within us. It's not just in some of us; it's in everyone. And as we let our own light shine, we unconsciously give other people permission to do the same. As we are liberated from our own fear, our presence automatically liberates others.

ᕦ Marianne Williamson[1]

PART 1

UNIVERSAL PATTERNS OF LEADING IN UNCERTAIN TIMES

How do some people, organizations, and coalitions thrive in uncertain times? What enables them to appear so certain and take decisive action amid ambiguity about the future?

Yogi Berra was right when he said, "The future ain't what it used to be." Not much else is certain these days. Steady state now is changing at the speed of the environment. This frightens, overwhelms, and immobilizes some people. For others, this global reset is a thrill ride and they want a front seat. If this sounds like you, the PRIMES in Part 1 will get you outfitted to "make your dent in the universe."

Here's the deal. Almost all the tame problems have been solved. We get to solve the wicked problems. Wicked problems affect a lot of people and it takes a lot of people, all with their own agendas, to collaborate and solve them. In this context, "a lot" means more than seven. When fewer than seven people can solve a problem, even if it is technically complex, they can self-organize and get the job done. Once the group size exceeds seven, the social dynamic switches from small group behavior to large group behavior. Large groups quickly become dysfunctional, are unsustainable, and do not produce meaningful, lasting outcomes unless led. Sorry to break this news to all you "new agers," but I have tried almost every trendy idea about emergent and self-organizing systems over the last three decades, and have concluded that groups with more than seven members need to be led.

The people who, amid uncertainty, successfully lead large problem-solving groups share three characteristics. First, they are clear about what they are up to and how they spend their precious time. Second, they are intentional and willing to go first. Finally, they have mastered the art of enrolling others to join them. The nine PRIMES revealed in the three chapters of Part 1 will outfit you with these capabilities.

Your own mind is a sacred enclosure into which nothing harmful can enter except by your promotion.

ᴥ Ralph Waldo Emerson[1]

CHAPTER 1

BEING CLEAR ON WHAT'S REALLY IMPORTANT

How did you decide how you spent your time yesterday? What criteria are you using to allocate your time tomorrow?

What do you stand for? What are you leading toward? How do you decide the best way to spend your time? What would your life be like if your answers to these questions were perfectly clear? The PRIMES called "LEADING," "IN–ON," and "CHANGE VERSUS TRANSFORMATION" will give you clarity about these fundamental questions. After you are outfitted with these three PRIMES, your calendar will never look the same. You will be selective about which meeting requests you choose to accept or decline. You will have a crystal clear rationale for why you are doing what you are doing and not doing what you are not doing. From this place of clarity, you will access ways to make more significant and meaningful contributions to groups and organizations of which you are a part and communities that you serve, using less effort.

The best is he who calls men to the best. And those who heed the call are also blessed. But worthless who call not, heed not, but rest.

           ✎ Hesiod[1]
eighth century BCE Greek poet

Set Direction

Align Resources

Inspire Action

**Be Responsible
for Results**

LEADING

LEADING

Does being called a "leader" mean you are "leading"?
What does "leading" mean?

Amazon.com currently sells 13,391 books on leadership. So why are people not leading effectively? Do we make it too complex? The LEADING PRIME defines the act of leading as setting direction, allocating resources, and inspiring action. Any time you are not doing these three things, you are not leading. Now let's put this distinction into context by looking at six words: three nouns and three verbs. First, the nouns:

Leader: A title

Manager: A title

Operator: A title

These three words convey what people *are*. They do not dictate or even indicate what a person of any given title actually does.

Now let's look at three verbs:

Leading: Setting direction, allocating resources, inspiring action, and being accountable for results

Managing: Balancing capacity with demand and ensuring predictable value is created using an efficient system

Operating: Using the system as designed to produce value

These words convey what people *do*. They specifically indicate an action. Acting in any of these three ways is not determined by what you are called. Many of us who are called leaders spend most of our time managing and operating. I also see, at times, people who are called managers and operators leading.

Take a moment to highlight the times over the last five days when you were setting direction, aligning resources, and inspiring action. Do the same for your boss (if you have one). Here are some tips to help you do an honest assessment. If you own a law firm, when you were practicing law, you were operating your business. If you are cutting hair in the salon you own, you are operating your business. If you own a consulting firm and you are consulting, you are operating your business. When you spend your time doing what the business does, you are not leading. Even when you spend your time making your business more efficient, you are managing, not leading, your business.

So, if you are like most of us, you will notice, looking back over the last week or so, that the attraction to manage and operate is very strong. This type of work is more certain and less risky. Leading is ambiguous and offers terrific opportunity to look bad in front of others.

I am not suggesting that there is a right answer to your allocation of time across these three activities. I am saying that unless the organization you are part of is perfectly suited for its future, people have to spend time leading. The question is, "Are the right people (including you) spending the right amount of time leading versus managing and operating?"

Discipline is remembering what you want.

                   ❧ David Campbell[2]

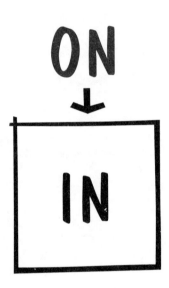

IN—ON

IN–ON

Are you seduced by working "in" the business at the expense of "on" it?

The IN–ON PRIME enables people to distinguish between working IN the business from working ON the business. Most people, especially leaders and managers, spend too much time in the operation and far too little time working on it.[3]

When working IN your business, you operate the systems and solve the problems that already exist. When you work ON your business, your activities either change or transform it; you bring forth new ways for the business to operate and produce extraordinary results (or failure) in the market. The power of this PRIME is unleashed once you recognize that at any time, you are either working IN your business or ON your business. IN isn't ON and there's no overlap.

Working "ON" the Business	**Working "IN" the Business**
Imagining the business as it will be	Operating the business as it is
Setting strategic direction	Implementing strategy
Establishing budget	Managing budget
Establishing hiring criteria	Hiring people
Transforming the system	Making the current system run better
Identifying new markets	Servicing the current market
What are we going to do next?	How can we do what we are doing better?
Determining what customers to serve	Servicing existing customers
Causing creative tension	Resolving creative tension

IN is seductive, whereas ON is ambiguous and scary. IN provides rich opportunities for leaders to take control, save the day, and earn expressions of praise and awe from staff and peers. ON carries inherent risk of being wrong and embarrassed and even shamed. IN wants all of the leader's attention and is threatened when he or she takes time to work ON the business. As long as IN keeps a leader's attention, nothing changes. Anyone can work IN a business, but if leaders don't work ON their business, neither will anyone else. The organization can't grow and any complex problem solving, change, or transformation effort will fail.

Over lunch one day with my friend Kai Dosier, I commented on how frustrating it was that our company had not broken through the $10 million revenue barrier. My team and I continually approached the target, retracted, and repeated the pattern. Everyone worked hard, and I was mystified as to why we hadn't yet succeeded. In the center of a napkin, Kai sketched the illustration at the start of this section of the book. When he finished, Kai looked at me and said, "Leaders typically short-change the time they devote to working ON the business." Then he asked, "Are you spending enough time working ON your business?"

Immediately, I began to distinguish my IN from my ON activities over the previous days. It became clear that I spent almost all of my time as a consultant—at work IN the business. When I helped my clients work ON their businesses, I was at work IN my own. Over the next several days, I realized where my choices had led me. Kai also turned me on to Michael Gerber's book *The E-Myth Revisited*. It further illuminated the distinction between the competing interests of IN and ON activities. Kai's napkin sketch stuck in my mind, and I could no longer ignore the lopsided amount of time I was allocating to working IN my business rather than ON it.

Yet in the days that followed, I noticed that I continued to spend most of my time at work IN the business. I found that I was easily distracted from work ON my business by some bright and shiny opportunity that popped up and gave me an opportunity to run to the rescue. A client needed me. Issues with the staff cried for attention. "Once-in-a-lifetime" opportunities demanded to be chased! I began to recognize that "only I can do it" and "this chance will never come again" were myths; they provided convenient excuses to avoid the relatively ambiguous responsibility of leading change. Self-deception kept me entrenched in the status quo. By working IN my business, I avoided learning how to lead and build a company. Once I began to work ON my business and gave it the leadership attention it needed, it grew at a sustained 35 percent growth rate, and I eventually sold it for a handsome profit.

The IN–ON distinction applies to managers, supervisors, and individuals, not just owners and senior leaders. However, most organizational cultures allow very little room for ON work. For major transformations to succeed, people at every level of the organization must be doing ON work, not just maintaining the status quo.

In looking back over more than 25 years of working with many different leaders, I've concluded that the failure to recognize the distinction between IN and ON—mismanagement of the critical allocation of time and attention to each—is the number one reason why change and transformation efforts fail. I have found myself drawing the concept on scraps of paper in the halls of the nation's capitol, on the plains of Iowa, and in the inner cities of Kenya. The IN–ON PRIME may be the most important one to master in order to drive successful change and transformation, create the future, and produce extraordinary results.

There is no set formula for how much energy to give either IN or ON, but without taking some time to work ON the business and to build this PRIME into the culture, leaders cannot gain the perspective necessary to get above the day-to-day craziness and use the PRIMES to chart the way forward to success.

For more on this subject, I encourage you to get a copy of Michael Gerber's book *E-Myth Revisited*.

The future is largely subject to our creation.

୨ Dr. Russell Ackoff[4]

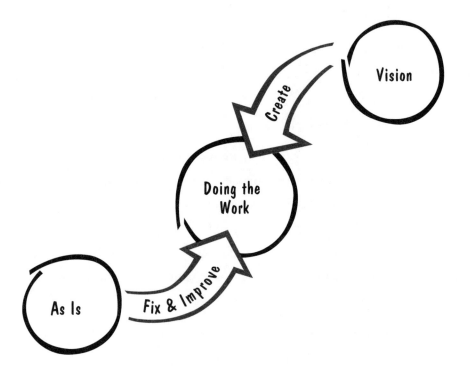

CHANGE VERSUS TRANSFORMATION

CHANGE versus TRANSFORMATION

Are you fixing or creating?

Does solving your problem require CHANGE or TRANSFORMATION? Both are difficult, but there are critical distinctions leaders often don't realize until it's too late. CHANGE is the right path when a problem is relatively simple and the current system needs only a tune-up. TRANSFORMATION is the right path when problems are "wicked" and a completely new system is required. Mastery begins by choosing the right path.

CHANGE requires you to become familiar with the current situation and to work to make things better, faster, cheaper, or some other "-er" word. Success is judged by efficiencies and economies that are realized at the end of our effort compared with where we started. When we choose change, our future is really a reconditioned or improved version of the past.

TRANSFORMATION involves a break with the past that is traumatic but potentially freeing. In transforming, we design our future and invent ways to bring it into reality. Transformation doesn't describe our future by referencing the past (better, faster, or cheaper); it births a future that is entirely new.

Transformation is the only means by which a man landed on the moon. In 1961, President John F. Kennedy declared, "I believe this nation should commit itself to achieving the goal, before this decade is out, of landing a man on the Moon and returning him safely to Earth." Engineers were clear that no improvements to the Gemini space program would realize this vision, so they invented Apollo. Apollo wasn't a better Gemini. It was an entirely new system. President Kennedy's declaration outlined all the necessary components of a transformation:

- Crystal clear objective

- Specific outcome

- Certain date

From that declaration a new world was created.

I have had the distinct privilege of being present at moments of transformation. One that comes to mind occurred in a conference room at Consol Energy in Pittsburgh, Pennsylvania. Consol is an energy company that focuses on extracting coal and gas. This work is inherently risky. The top team was committed to cutting its accident rates every year and accomplished that goal for several years in a row. This company had the best safety record in the business. On this particular day, we were trying to figure out how we could "improve" the safety record for the next year. We had established a goal that we thought was in our grasp.

Then one of the senior executives of Consol, Nick Deluliis, came to the front of the room and pointed to the recently agreed-to goal. He asked the group what this number meant to them. People said it was an achievable goal but would take a lot of work and focus by the managers. They also felt it would create a new standard in the industry. Nick looked everyone square in the eyes and said that to him "the goal meant the group was willing to tolerate someone getting hurt." He went on to suggest that rather than being "safer" when compared with Consol's past or the industry at large, why not simply declare that "working at Consol Energy is safe," period?

From this transformative perspective, what instantly showed up were all the aspects of the business that were not perfectly safe. These exposures became apparent as violations of the statement, "Working at Consol is safe." So people in the room began to say, "Well we can't say that because (fill in the blank)," to which Nick responded, "Well then that is what we need to work on and eliminate right now because these types of exposures have no place in a Consol that is 'now' safe." Can you imagine, upon return to their work settings deep in mines and hanging off the sides of mountains, what these managers and supervisors saw? Through the transformative lens of "Consol is safe now," they saw everything that was not safe. And they dealt with it relentlessly. Consol leads a nation that leads the world in being safe whilst doing an inherently hazardous job. China has 20 times more deaths and injuries than the United States. My hope is that a group in China takes a stand now for transforming its extraction industry by declaring it "safe now" and doing whatever it takes to live into that transformative declaration.

Put this PRIME in action. Ask your group or organization, "What determines what they're doing right now?" Is it about making a better, faster, cheaper past, or committing to fulfill a declaration and create a future? It's one or the other, but never both. Ignore this distinction at your peril.

Each path has unique hazards and challenges, and requires unique tools. Tools of change are embodied in corporate improvement programs like Activity Based Costing, Six Sigma, and others.[5] These tools are effective when a better past is the desired outcome, but they're dead weight in the business of transformation.

We elect leaders because they promise change. Yet issues like health care, energy, climate, and security cry out for transformation. When things don't work out, these leaders claim it's because we're on the wrong track.

The instruments of transformation are imagination, declaration, invention, and innovation; they require a childlike fascination with "mashing" things together to create something new. Both change and transformation compel the group to let go of the way things are. In a way, something very real is dying. The familiar system will no longer exist, and with it goes many memories, both positive and negative. And this familiarity is being traded for an unknown future. These feelings are much stronger around transformation than around change. In transformation, it can seem to people that the very soul of the system or organization is at risk. Oftentimes these feelings are valid. To manage the resistance this fear can generate, it is essential to make clear the good that is possible if the change or transformation is successful and the certain bad that happens if you fail. This principle is crucial and will be handled in more detail later in this chapter.

So far I have focused the discussion of "CHANGE VERSUS TRANSFORMATION" in a context of business and groups. Know that everything regarding CHANGE VERSUS TRANSFORMATION applies to you as an individual. Are you "trying to lose weight" or are you "choosing the healthy alternative at every option"? Are you "trying to quit smoking" or are you "living smoke free"? Are you "trying to get better at being your word" or are you "being a person of integrity"? As long as you are "trying" to do something, you are "not doing" something. As long as you are "doing this so that you can have or be that," you are "not having or being that." Here is something you personally can take on right now as a rule in your life: Be a person who never says "try."

I was transformed at Queenstown Golf Club on Chesapeake Bay. My playing partner was an old friend named Dave Kolanda. We both started our careers as engineers at IBM some 30 years ago. Somewhere in the round I casually mentioned that I had begun to write this book. Dave turned and said, "So you're an author." The statement struck me as odd. In the clubhouse, Dave struck up a conversation with the waiter and introduced me as "an author." It was clear to me that to this waiter, that is what I was. My past was irrelevant. It was my future that was giving me my name now. From that moment on, I truly enjoyed writing this book. After all, Dave had transformed me into an author by declaring me one, so I knew I'd better act like one and write.

Notice the people around you. Are they working to fix the past or live into a vision of the future? Are they even aware there is a difference? Many choose change even when they recognize that transformation is necessary. Experience has shown me that these people carry a limiting belief that tells them that powerful declarations should never be made in the absence of precise clarity—the ability to see not only the future in precise detail but also every detail of how to get to that future.

For these people, transformation is simply too big a step. It requires information beyond what they currently know or know how to find.

Such "clarity" is not only unnecessary, it is limiting.

Through the lens of the three PRIMES revealed in this chapter—LEADING, IN-ON, and CHANGE VERSUS TRANSFORMATION—you can now distinguish how you are spending your time. You are clear on when you are leading and when you are not. You can recognize when you are working on the business. And you will be certain when you are standing for change or transformation. There is no wrong or right answer; there is only the truth that your priorities are not what they say they are. Your priorities are where you choose to spend your time. Access the needs of your team, group, organization, or community at large. What kind of "you" are they crying out for? Listen. Then be what they need.

In Chapter 2, you will be outfitted with the three PRIMES that will enable you to act boldly and powerfully.

The dogmas of the quiet past are inadequate to the stormy present. The occasion is piled high with difficulty, and we must rise with the occasion. As our case is new, so we must think anew, and act anew. We must disenthrall ourselves, and then we shall save our country.

❧ Abraham Lincoln, December 1, 1862, in Message to Congress[6]

CHAPTER 2

BEING INTENTIONAL AND GOING FIRST

What are you committed to making happen and by when? What does "committed" mean? What does your commitment mean to others?

You are now outfitted with the LEADING, IN–ON, and CHANGE versus TRANSFORMATION PRIMES. You are now a person who clearly knows what he or she is doing and what he or she is not doing with respect to leading, working on systems, and causing change or transformation. Each week, when you plan how you will use your time, you are actively and intentionally allocating your time to either running or improving the current system or creating a whole new system At this point, you are dangerous to the status quo.

Now that you can rightly allocate your time, how do you make the most of it? Chapter 2 is about acting boldly and powerfully in a way that inspires others to follow.

What is it about some people who seem to be able to attract the best and brightest to help them accomplish so much? They have an air of confidence about them, even in the midst of uncertainty and ambiguity. You may be one of them. If so, the next three PRIMES will validate what you already know. If you admire someone like this, the PRIMES that follow will outfit you to access untapped power within yourself and use that power to make things happen.

Simply let your "Yes" be "Yes," and your "No," "No."

                              ❧ Matthew 5:37[1]

SAY ⟹ DO

INTEGRITY

INTEGRITY

Does your "yes" really mean "yes"?

Leave all other connotations of INTEGRITY aside for a moment. In the context of the PRIMES, INTEGRITY means, "I say what I am going to do, and I do what I say... every time." INTEGRITY is not based on values or morals. It is based on honoring and keeping your word. When people choose to operate in INTEGRITY, their words about the future cause the future. People trust them. They reach a level of performance that otherwise would be unattainable.

There is very little integrity in the world. Manufacturers make claims about their products that are unfulfilled. Doctors say they will see you at 11:00 a.m. Mechanics say your car will be ready in the morning and the cost will be $200. A coworker says he will have the report ready by noon. Government leaders say they will act in the best interest of the country. But products fail to function as advertised. Doctors have "waiting" rooms. Repairs cost more and take longer. Coworkers often disappoint us. And government leaders act in their own best interests. Is this always the case? No, but it is sometimes, and integrity is an all-or-nothing game.

Zig Ziglar said, "The most important persuasion tool you have in your entire arsenal is integrity."[2] Choosing to live in integrity is the greatest commitment you can make to those around you. INTEGRITY is an essential value of high-performance groups.

At the outset of any project, I ask the people involved to live in integrity for the duration of the project. The rule is that there are no small or big promises; there are only promises. And all promises will be kept. No other PRIME evokes such a visceral response. I'm no longer surprised by how much the invitation to live with integrity terrifies people. It's not easy to be true to our word, but what's the alternative? Do you want to scale an exposed cliff with the person on the other end of the rope watching out for you . . . sometimes . . . maybe? Do you want to be involved in a project in which deadlines become "guidelines" and meetings start "around" nine o'clock?

To live in INTEGRITY with those around you requires three skills:

1.   You must recognize when you have been requested to, or are about to, give your word.

2.   Say "yes" only when you mean it. You should only say "yes" if you mean it.

3.   Get very good at saying "no," because that is going to be your most common response.

Integrity is the source of trust. Trust enables intimacy. If you get nothing else out of this book, get INTEGRITY. Embed integrity into your life and in the groups and teams of which you are a part. It is simple. Explain what it means. Commit to having it.

Until one is committed there is hesitancy, the chance to draw back, always ineffectiveness. Concerning all acts of initiative (and creation), there is one elementary truth the ignorance of which kills countless ideas and splendid plans: that the moment one definitely commits oneself the providence moves too. A whole stream of events issues from the decision, raising in one's favor all manner of unforeseen incidents, meetings and material assistance, which no man could have dreamt would come his way. I learned a deep respect for one of Goethe's couplets: "Whatever you can do or dream you can, begin it. Boldness has genius, power, and magic in it!"

☙ W. H. Murray[3]

TRUST THE UNIVERSE

Is your vision limited to what you've already seen?

Groups typically create visions based on what they already know. Some groups take the next step, and create visions that are dependent on learning things they know they don't already know. Real visionaries do the following:

- Understand that most of what is needed is available in the universe; they do not know what they do not know.

- Believe that whatever they need to realize—whatever vision they declare—is out there in the future somewhere.

- Trust that the universe will make available whatever the visionary needs.

Visualize beyond what you know.

There is also a dark side to TRUST THE UNIVERSE. When I interviewed leaders for this book, I introduced the PRIMES to them in the form of cards laid out on a table, with one PRIME on each card. I invited them to select a few that "jumped out" at them.

Dennis Whittle, founder of a cutting-edge, Web-based social entrepreneurship firm called Global Giving, quickly selected five PRIMES and gave me his thoughts on the first four.[4] With the last card still in his hand, he hesitated and began to tap it on the table a bit too hard. His eyes welled up, which is uncharacteristic of him. He held up the TRUST THE UNIVERSE card and said, "This one is schlock!" I knew more was coming, so I stayed quiet. "TRUST THE UNIVERSE is a myth," he continued. "It's a required myth, an essential myth for any true leader, but a myth just the same. Embracing this PRIME is the only real way to create transformative possibilities."

"Every leader [had] better get this," Dennis said. "Only sometimes, after you make your bold declaration, you have to take out a second mortgage while you wait for the universe to show up. And sometimes, not only does the universe not show up, you lose your house. For every change agent entrepreneur with the Midas touch, for every tale of glory, there are a hundred stories of 'everything ventured, nothing gained.'"

The truth about TRUST THE UNIVERSE is there's no guarantee of success, no matter how bold or noble the declaration. People get hurt. They risk everything, and some lose everything, every day. There are no secret codes, and every revolutionary leader who stands up to regale an audience with "The Formula" for unfettered success does so in retrospect.

TRUST THE UNIVERSE isn't about finding faith and being assured of success. Without a doubt, there are people who put no stock in the universe and have achieved positions of wealth and notoriety. For a leader to ignore Providence and all its potential, however, is foolish. Great leaders struggle with the same challenges, frustrations, doubts, setbacks, and humiliations as everyone else. Leaders understand that although TRUST THE UNIVERSE promises no guarantees, it gives us the ability to imagine without limit and watch what shows up.

At the beginning of this book, I acknowledged people without whose help I'd never have been able to complete *The PRIMES*. And yet when I publicly declared I was going to publish this book, I didn't even know that some of them were out there. Thank you, universe!

Do or do not; there is no try.

                                 ❧ Yoda[5]

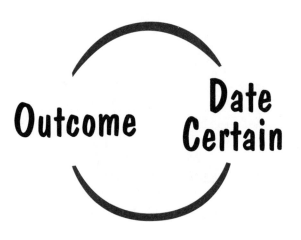

DECLARATION

DECLARATION

Are you willing to live unreasonably?

A DECLARATION is a statement of "what" will be achieved by "when."[6] One of the most profound privileges I've experienced is to witness a group DECLARE to achieve a clear outcome by a specific date. President Kennedy's DECLARATION was *an American to the moon and back by the end of the decade.* Mahatma Gandhi's was *a free India before my death.* Babe Ruth's was *the next pitch over the wall.* These leaders pointed then hit. Athletes today swing away. When they happen to hit one over the wall, they stand and point. That is not declarative leadership. The order matters.

When a DECLARATION is made with INTEGRITY, *the language itself shifts from passive to powerful:*

Passive Voice	→	Powerful Voice
Plan	→	Declare
Try	→	Do
I should	→	I shall
I'm going to	→	I am
We ought to	→	We are
But / If	→	Regardless
I support the effort	→	I commit to the outcome
With conditions	→	Unconditionally
Soon	→	Now

I recently was involved in a transformation project for a very large logistics system. In this context, think of logistics as moving the right things at the right time from the makers and suppliers to the customers and consumers. This system is massive; the biggest logistics system in the world. It is really a system of systems. There are many subsystems, each with its own owner, and no single authority over the whole thing. At the outset of the project, it was estimated that the system was operating at a minimum of 30 percent inefficiency. Most thought this was a conservative assessment. Real breakthrough required that leaders from many different organizations freely chose to join together a coalition of the willing. However, trust was low among the major players.

Rather than go to a ropes course or engage in other team-building experiences, we decided to "meet in the work." We picked five problems that obviously needed to be solved. We described an outcome for each of the projects and established a specific, date-certain deadline. We set up teams to get the work done. As is usually the case, the teams spent most of their time figuring things out and then asked for more time to actually get the outcome accomplished. The leadership group refused. There would be *no* changing the deadline. This was an unexpected and almost unprecedented response. The teams were at the same time shocked, skeptical, and excited. The teams came back to leadership and said, "If you really want this outcome by that date, this is what must happen." And the leaders said, "Okay."

Three teams finished ahead of the deadline. Two teams were in serious trouble. Politics had crept into the conversation. People stopped playing fair. Their proposed solution would require power to be shifted, and the resisting forces were mounting. The team members did not feel that they had sufficient authority to resolve the impasse. Both teams skeptically brought their issues to the coalition of leaders. There were so many "reasons" why things should stay the way they were. The proposed new way might cause some unintended consequences. Status Quo was screaming out, "Do not do this until we are sure. Slow down!" In the past, it was at this point that leaders ducked and winked and sent the team back for more analysis. This time, something unusual happened.

The affected leaders got on the phone and cut a deal. It was intense and painful. But they felt they had to because they gave their word in front of the teams that the outcome would be realized on time. One deal was cut just hours before the deadline. The teams were shocked. This agreement just did not happen in the past. What they were witnessing is called "declarative leadership." They were shocked because although the world is crying out for it, declarative leadership is in very short supply. All five teams delivered the intended outcomes on time.

We had a party and gave out awards. Something more than the outcomes was being celebrated. Leaders had led. Teams produced. Integrity ruled. Outcomes were created on time. The organization realized new possibilities. The leaders and the teams were hungry for more. This happened because of the powerful combination of a DECLARATION made with INTEGRITY.

If your actions inspire others to dream more, learn more, do more, and become more, you are a leader.

                                                   John Quincy Adams[7]

CHAPTER 3

ENROLLING OTHERS

Can you call people, from disenfranchisement and mere compliance,
to their highest level of commitment?

You are clear about your goals. You have boldly declared that you will achieve a specific outcome by a certain date, with integrity. You know that you need others to commit to work with you in order to accomplish this declaration, since there are not many worthy outcomes that you—or any single individual—could produce on his or her own. This chapter will show you how powerful leaders and managers enroll groups of people in the risky business of problem solving, change, and transformation. One PRIME will show you how to get the folks to lean into your vision. The next will show you how to compel the group to do whatever it takes. The third reveals how to generate unprecedented power within the group.

I stress again that I am deliberately using the word "group" as opposed to "team." This is because while all teams are groups, not all groups are teams. Teams are groups in which the feeling is one-for-all-and-all-for-one. Teams are willing to wear the same t-shirts, and have a common objective and sense of what winning looks like. Teams have someone to whom they all report and who can tell them what to do. Teams are a luxury. But many groups you will be leading and of which you're a member are more like coalitions. The problems you'll solve and the change you'll drive will increasingly require that strangers, competitors, cautious allies, and suspicious stakeholders participate and commit. Those who master leading these heterogeneous coalitions will never be without a purpose—or a paycheck.

The desire and pursuit of the whole is called love.

೨ Plato[1]

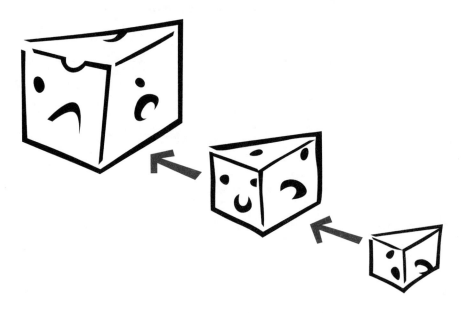

DYNAMIC INCOMPLETENESS

DYNAMIC INCOMPLETENESS

*Can you create a vision that is compelling because of what it says
and at the same time inviting—for what it leaves yet to be said?*

"Without vision the people shall perish." So said King Solomon approximately 2,500 years ago. Today's top CEOs agree. They cite "engaging employees in the company vision" as one of their top priorities while admitting how hard this is to do. Leaders are responsible for creating vision that informs the strategic direction and inspires the people to act.

The truth of the matter is that creating visions frightens leaders. They are afraid that people might not like their vision and will accuse them of being a bad leader. In truth, the worst leaders take no responsibility for creating a vision. They either ignore it altogether or they delegate the job to lower ranks under the management façade of empowerment. Slightly better leaders bring too much vision forward and demand that you buy into it completely and get inspired fast—because they think it is wonderful.

Great leaders build visions using the principle revealed in the DYNAMIC INCOMPLETENESS PRIME. They know it is their job to go first and bring some vision forward. They make clear the elements of the vision that they consider to be the most important and exciting. It is just as important for a leader to make clear what is incomplete in his or her vision. The leader then requests that the rest of the group bring forward any ideas that fit within the overall framework and fill in the missing parts resulting in a description of a future that people literally fall in love with.

Building visions following the DYNAMIC INCOMPLETENESS PRIME does a number of positive things. It

1.   Enables leaders to bring something forward first yet frees them from feeling like they have to have all the answers,

2.   Creates a space and invitation to engage the entire group in cocreation of the vision, which then

3.   Allows access to all the ideas of the group, and

4.   Promotes co-ownership. The broad sense of "owning the vision" makes people willing to "act unreasonably" to achieve it.

DYNAMIC INCOMPLETENESS compels everyone to cocreate the vision because there are always more holes to fill. People develop a sense of ownership in what they help to create, which is the first value of this PRIME. Having members of the group own the vision makes it more likely to succeed.

DYNAMIC INCOMPLETENESS adheres to the truth that too much form causes resistance and too much void causes chaos. The leader's job is to bring just enough form to inspire the people and frame what needs to be articulated. In a nutshell, that is the art of visioning.

You must avoid constraining yourself to the misguided task of vision statements. The expansive idea (vision) crashes into the reductive idea (statement). Instead, you want to make your DYNAMICALLY INCOMPLETE vision marvelously expansive by lightly covering every aspect of the future that you can image. Expand your vision field to the point that it literally crowds out reality.

DYNAMIC INCOMPLETENESS is a powerful way for you to TRUST THE UNIVERSE. What you don't know creates the invitation and the space for others to join you to bring forward information and ideas that you couldn't have imagined. As others invest in your vision, encourage them to follow your lead by filling in the holes. As they engage in DYNAMIC INCOMPLETENESS with you, they'll fill in what they can and leave room for others to do the rest.

When you are inspired by some great purpose, some extraordinary project, all your thoughts break their bonds: Your mind transcends limitations, your consciousness expands in every direction, and you find yourself in a new, great, and wonderful world. Dormant forces, faculties, and talents become alive, and you discover yourself to be a greater person by far than you ever dreamed yourself to be.

ও Patanjali[2]

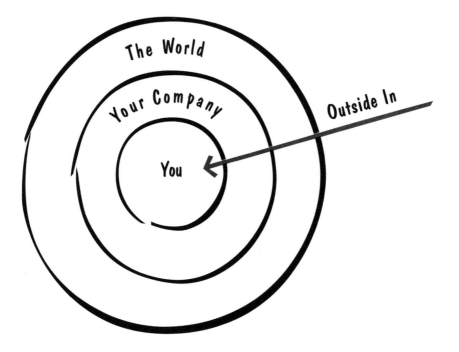

ENNOBLEMENT

ENNOBLEMENT

Does your vision elevate people in degree and excellence and respect and inspire them to act boldly?

ENNOBLEMENT may be the most commonly violated PRIME. Here are the most common ways to violate the ENNOBLEMENT PRIME:

- Start your vision out by making statements about yourself or your company.

- Use the future tense.

- Strive to make a vision statement.

Visions that ennoble begin by painting a picture of the world at large and the community your business serves. This picture is a present-tense description of a desired future state. Ennobling visions are comprehensive in scope to the degree that they crowd out reality.

A blatant example of disregard for the ENNOBLEMENT PRIME is evident in the first sentence of Enron's vision statement: "Enron's vision is to become the world's leading energy company . . . ." The vision begins with the company talking about itself. And it does so in a future tense. And we all saw what that got them!

A health care provider recently brought its vision into alignment with the ENNOBLEMENT PRIME. Its vision changed from one that started out saying:

> (Name of company) will be the health care provider of choice within the context of the state of California's new fiscal realities.

To one that followed the ENNOBLEMENT PRIME:

> At (Name of company), we see the people of California equipped to make the best choices when in need of health care services. Their alternatives and the trade-offs are clear. Should they need it, assistance is a phone call away, 24 hours a day, in any language. No matter what their financial circumstance, they know they are getting all the right information and feel empowered and capable of making an anxiety-free, fully informed decision on how they want to proceed. We, the people of (Name of company), make this possible by providing (details of solution they intend to deliver in the future.)

Notice that the second version begins with a vision for people whom the company serves and then moves to define the company's role in making that vision happen for its customers. Also notice the tense in the second version. Visions that ENNOBLE are always described in the present tense.

How do we build visions that ennoble and empower people? Start with the fact that the ennobling vision must be larger than you, your team, or even your organization. Let's use the illustration of the ENNOBLEMENT PRIME:

- Do not begin with yourself or your organization but instead with the world—the largest possible frame of reference. Imagine this world in a manner that inspires and motivates your team.

- Describe your group's role in this imagined world and how your team will serve its needs.

- Then imagine what you and your group need to do to make the vision real.

Powerful visions are developed from the outside in and answer the question, "What do I stand for outside in the world we serve, as opposed to inside our own organization?" Visions provide direction when the way forward is unclear. They create a context for daily activities and lend meaning to every process encompassed by the vision, no matter how menial or challenging. People don't become ennobled by building an organization for the organization's sake. It happens when they see themselves as an essential part of a group that is doing something wonderful for its community and the world.

The power of ennoblement can be seen in the following story[3]:

> An Irish priest walks along a road where laborers are busy on a cool foggy morning. The first group of workers were grumbling and their workplace was disheveled. The priest asked the men what they were doing, and the foreman replied, "Me and the boys are making bricks, Father—fast as we can. Can't really stop to talk, no disrespect, gotta mix this sand and rock to make bricks; a lot of bricks." The priest bid them good work and continued on his walk.
>
> A little ways away, the priest came upon a second group. It looked like the same operation as the first group, but the job site was tidier and the men seemed more content and moved with a deeper sense of purpose than the first group. Again the priest greeted them and again asked what they were doing. The foreman smiled and said, "Father, we're helping to make walls. Right now we're mixing sand and water and rocks to make the bricks for that crew up there on the north side of the building. The priest blessed their work and continued down the road. As he walked, he began to hear joyous singing and laughing. As rounded the bend, he came upon a third group of laborers. It looked like the same operation that the other two groups were doing. But the site was immaculate. The bricks were stacked squarely. The men worked in a collective rhythm. As the priest arrived, the men stopped and greeted him warmly. "Good morning men," the priest said. "And what would you be doing today?" "Ah, Father, today is a true blessing for the Lord. Today we are

building a house of God. When we are done, our village will come and worship here for generations. Right now we are helping to make the walls. Our part of that is to mix the rock, sand, and water to make the bricks, and a true labor of love it is."

The first crew saw themselves only as brick makers. The second team saw their brick-making work as an integral part of making a wall—that greater context, creating a more meaningful perspective that results in their desire to make quality products. The third group was clearly enrolled in an ennobling vision and saw their work as integral to something wonderful. This ennoblement caused them to work and produce at the highest level.

To tap into the human desire to participate in something meaningful sets free an almost miraculous power source that compels us to go beyond the limits we perceive today. If you waste this resource, you deny others the opportunity to accomplish amazing things.

Power, n.

1. Ability to act, regarded as latent or inherent; the faculty of doing or performing something; capacity for action or performance; capability of producing an effect, whether physical or moral.

ço American Dictionary of the English Language
Noah Webster, 1877

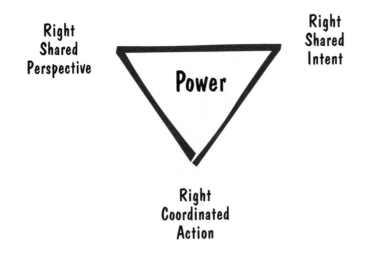

POWER

POWER

Do you know how to turn strangers, competitors, cautious allies,
and suspicious stakeholders into powerful, outcome-driven coalitions?

Any group's power is a function of (1) the degree to which its members are willing to operate from a shared perspective, (2) the degree to which they will commit to a shared intent, and (3) the level of coordination of their actions. A weakness in any part of the triangle erodes the power.

Power is one of three ways to get something accomplished, along with authority and force. The source of the energy is what distinguishes each of the three.

1. *Force* gets members of the group to do something because they are intimidated by your sheer strength. The energy of force comes from the simple fact that you can beat others up if they do not comply.

2. *Authority* requires that you compel someone to do something because you have been empowered by a larger community to enforce its will. The energy of authority is generated outside the group and delegated to one who then uses it to get the group to act in a specific manner.

3. *Power* is energy that is generated from within the group by the group itself when members freely choose to work collectively toward a common outcome. The group also chooses to empower its leader to work in the group's best interest.

The POWER PRIME reveals the components required to generate unprecedented levels of power. Leaders must set their sights on mastering the skill of generating power in groups as opposed to teams. Teams are only one kind of group, and their future is limited. Globalization, interconnectedness, and systems thinking are producing an entirely new level of problems and possibilities that no single organization or authority can get its arms around. The highest skill to master is the ability to generate power in groups composed of strangers, competitors, cautious allies, and suspicious stakeholders. This is the world in which we live.

Power is not abstract; you can measure it by analytically asking individual members of the group three sets of questions to quantify the level of power the group is generating. The more power available, the more the group can accomplish.

Part 2 will provide you with nine PRIMES that are essential for generating group power. These will enable you to turn any group of strangers, competitors, cautious allies, and suspicious stakeholders into powerful, outcome-driven coalitions. These PRIMES are simple, but they are not simplistic. Many readers have told me that they find themselves re-reading this section as they're forced to lead in uncertain times.

We now know what power is, and we know why generating power in groups is so important to our future. Let's now get outfitted to generate it in any situation in which we might find ourselves.

When you try to pick out anything by itself, we find it hitched to everything else in the Universe.

John Muir[4]

PART 2

UNIVERSAL PATTERNS OF POWERFUL ALLIANCES

How do you generate unprecedented power within the group? Is this question all that important to you?

The future belongs to those who can turn strangers, competitors, cautious allies, and suspicious stakeholders into powerful, problem-solving, outcome-driven alliances and coalitions. Part 2 presents nine PRIMES that reveal specifically how to have any group of disparate individuals embrace a shared perspective, common intent, and synchronized action. This will give your group access to unprecedented power sufficient to overcome ruthless resistance to changing the status quo. You and your group will need every bit of power you can generate. Consider the fact that well over half of projects with high stakeholder complexity fail outright, while the rest go over cost and schedule significantly.[1]

Of the few projects that are finished, half fail to meet even the minimum expectations set forth at the outset. Most of this carnage is the result of failing to "go slow to go fast." Groups are in such a hurry to take action that they do not take the time to establish the right shared perspective and true commitment to the right shared intent. While this tendency to take action may get you "off the blocks" sooner, implementation will stall as people begin to question underlying assumptions—and even the intent and necessity for the project.

Don't contribute to this trend. Go slow to go fast. Master the nine PRIMES in Part 2, and you will join a very small group of people who actually joined up and solved a complex problem, drove a successful change process, or caused a valuable system-wide transformation.

Creating a new theory is not like destroying an old barn and erecting a skyscraper in its place. It is rather like climbing a mountain, gaining new and wider views, discovering unexpected connections between our starting points and its rich environment. But the point from which we started out still exists and can be seen, although it appears smaller and forms a tiny part of our broad view gained by the mastery of the obstacles on our adventurous way up.

       ✎ Albert Einstein[2]

CHAPTER 4

GAINING SHARED PERSPECTIVE

Everyone claims to value diversity. Can maintaining
diverse perspectives ever be a bad thing?

Think of the term "perspective" as "the place from which one observes." If people are looking at a situation from different perspectives, they almost never agree on the presenting problem, root cause, consequences, or solution. People's perspectives set up their perception, and their perception dictates their reality. Then we fight over whose "reality" is right. This goes nowhere.

The three PRIMES revealed in this chapter break "perspective" into three dimensions: the angle, the level of abstraction, and the life cycle. Left to their own devices, individuals in groups tend to position themselves at different angles and levels of abstraction when they view a problem. They also start out with different beliefs regarding how close to the edge they are and how fast they are approaching it. Each person has a different sense of urgency.

The trick is to gather the individuals into a group so that they can look at and discuss the problem from various angles and levels together. Shared perspective enriches and sharpens the conversation, and is the first step in generating and accessing the group's full power.

Where you stand depends on where you sit.

✎ Miles' Law; Rufus E. Miles[1]

BLIND MEN AND THE ELEPHANT

BLIND MEN AND THE ELEPHANT

How do you help people to see the "whole thing"?

Countless people have heard the tale of the blind man who holds the elephant's trunk and has every reason to identify it as a snake. The same may be said for the blind man who stands next to the elephant's leg and perceives it to be a tree. The two men arrive at different conclusions because they have different information. Once members of a team observe this dynamic and recognize that they each hold only a *part* of the elephant, they often resolve their differences quickly.

A few years ago, I witnessed firsthand the awesome power of "seeing the elephant." The question at hand was, "Why were the responses to Hurricane Katrina and the Haitian earthquake such dismal failures?" After all, there are well-documented stories about these problems. During Katrina, ice sat melting in a stadium while people died from dehydration. After-action reports by the US government claim that with respect to the Haiti disaster response, well over 50 percent of the $1 billion spent by the US government alone was wasted. The issue we investigated was, "How did the good intentions of so many people and organizations result in such confusion and ineffectiveness?" It is important to note that responses to such large-scale events involve many governments and levels of governments, along with non-governmental groups like the Red Cross and private-sector companies—all of whom are trying to fix problems at the same time.

We began by interviewing many of the stakeholders and asking simple questions like the following:

- How would you describe the problems with the response to the disaster writ large?

- What was the root cause of the lack of coordination and the confusion?

- How did your organization and others contribute to the problems?

While the answers to these basic questions were all over the map, we unearthed a single key insight: that the collective group lacked a shared picture of the overall response. In other words, even the word "response" had different meanings, depending on which organization you asked.

Our solution was to gather everybody together and "draw a picture of the elephant." Once we had a shared, explicit representation of the "response," we were able to agree on the root causes of the problem and ways to make things go more smoothly moving forward. This outcome would not have been possible if we hadn't taken the time to gain a common picture of the entire system.

You don't have to be an artist to draw the "elephant," and the pictures do not need to be pretty. Simply get to a white board or grab a sheet of paper and draw a picture that answers the question, "How does this system work?" Do not be surprised if you end up with two to four different pictures; do not be discouraged if you have to crumple up many drafts before finding one that is useful. And always remember that the most important part of this process is the conversation you have during it. The picture, the "elephant," represents an explicit and shared model of how the system works. And there is a rule when building models: *All models are wrong. Some are useful*. A useful model is one that positions people at a common vantage point that allows them to discuss what they see—and how to affect it.

One last best practice: Do not delegate building the model to a third party. Build the model with the stakeholders directly. Codevelopment creates co-ownership of the model, and professional modelers love the model. And why let someone else have all the fun?

It isn't that they can't see the solution. It's that they can't see the problem.

                  ❧ G. K. Chesterton[2]

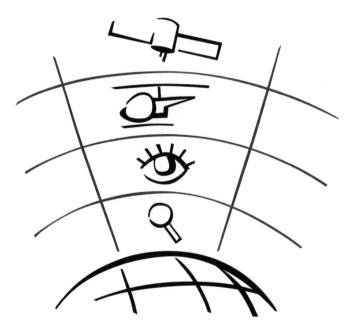

LEVELS OF PERSPECTIVE

LEVELS OF PERSPECTIVE

How do you help people to see the same "whole thing"?

The LEVELS OF PERSPECTIVE PRIME is similar to BLIND MEN AND THE ELEPHANT in that it is really about scope and abstraction. Depending on what you are trying to do, there is always an optimal level of perspective.

Consider this example:

You're stuck in traffic at an intersection. You're late for a meeting, frustrated and impatient, and look around in vain for a police officer to take control of the situation and get everyone moving. Once you tune the radio to the traffic channel, you learn that the cause of the backup is a broken-down truck miles ahead. Even if an officer were to arrive at your intersection, there would be little that he or she could do. The optimal level of perspective in this case is from high up. From this vantage point, cars become dots, and the primary and alternative paths for the flow of traffic become clear.

Now imagine you are the operator of the broken-down truck. A satellite view of the roads around you is of absolutely no value in your situation, since your problem requires a microscope approach. You need to go deeper and deeper into the truck to find the one thing that is broken and stopping the vehicle from running. The optimal frame of reference is tight.

Each individual in a group enters the problem-solving process already seeing the situation from some level of perspective and abstraction. The trick is to get everybody to share the optimal level of perspective.

It is usually best to begin with the big picture—an overall perspective like the one to be had from the satellite or helicopter in the previous example. When points of leverage (the car radio) and a problem's root cause (the news of an accident miles ahead) become apparent, you want to do your best to zoom in, as with a microscope, and address them.

Too often I see people use detailed management tools such as Six Sigma and Total Quality Management indiscriminately. While these programs can be extremely helpful, people frequently deploy them without bothering to determine where they will provide the greatest positive effect. As a result, they are too often used to shift problems from one management group to another. These "close-in" tools should only be used after the group has identified the root cause of the problem and the leverage points.

Choosing what you want to do, and when you want to do it, is an act of creation.

                                              ✒ Peter McWilliams[3]

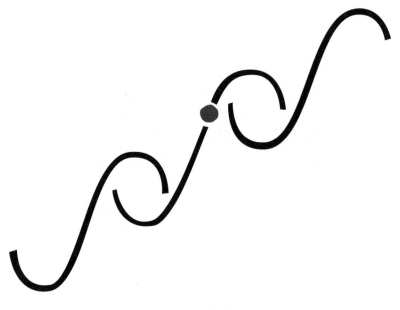

S-CURVES

S-CURVES

How do you lead people to a shared sense of now?

The S-CURVES PRIME has played a useful role in getting people to a shared perspective.[4] Specifically, it is a quick and effective way to get two or more people to a shared response to the questions "Do we need to change?" and "If we do need to change, how fast?"

I learned about this PRIME when I was supporting a large globalization project at Arthur Andersen back in the early 1990s. Charles Handy, then-visiting professor of the London Business School, illustrated the S-CURVE in a story and went on to apply the concept to Arthur Andersen.

An Irishman, a Story by Charles Handy

The story takes place around Dublin in an area having no signposts. Handy was lost in the hills behind Dublin and asked for directions. An old Irishman told him to follow the road to Dave's Bar. When he got there, well then, the road he wanted would be a quarter of a mile back and up to the right.

The S-CURVE is the story of every product, organization, relationship, and system. It is the story of history, of the Roman Empire, the American Empire, and of life itself. Just like these curves, every system has a time of "figuring it out," a period of growth, and then an inevitable collapse if no change is made. But there is hope: you can build a second curve before the first one goes down.

However, you have to get the new curve started before the first one even begins to peak. The paradox is that everything seems great just before the peak of the first curve. S-CURVE enables change leaders to state boldly, "If it's not broken, now might be the ideal time to jump to the next S-curve."

You can see S-curves everywhere because they affect everything. For example, take Microsoft's DOS operating system. Even if Microsoft continued to improve and develop DOS perfectly, would anyone really care? The IT environment around Microsoft evolved quickly. Microsoft was still making money on DOS when it jumped onto Windows—a well-timed jump, indeed, but one that caused the company to miss the optimum time to jump from Windows to the Internet. The company fell behind as AltaVista and NetScape came on the scene. Fortunately, Microsoft had the cash to get back in the game, but the jump was excessively expensive and the company lost market share. If IT companies have not already jumped into cloud computing and shared services, they are probably not long for this world—regardless of how much money they are currently making.

Most people and organizations wait until it is too late, until they are on the down side of the curve. But by then, the money or interest or even will is decreasing or gone.

So where are you and your group in terms of your current S-curve? It is important for you all to develop a shared perspective on this question.

You will use the same process for the S-CURVE PRIME as you did when drawing the elephant. Get everybody together and draw the S-CURVE PRIME; ask people to mark where they think the system is on it. After people make their initial marks, note the differences. Ask people who made marks at varying extremes to share their rationales with the group. I assure you the conversations will be extraordinary. Keep arguing until people have a shared perspective on where the system is on the S-curve. The effect on the group will be profound.

You dramatically increase the odds of getting what you want when you are clearer about what you want.

இ Peter DiGiammarino[5]

CHAPTER 5

ESTABLISHING SHARED INTENT

How do you lead the group to be intentional?

Shared intent represents the second corner of the POWER triangle. It is an unnatural state of group alignment about what outcome it stands for and will make happen by when, what is at stake if the group fails, and what can be gained if it succeeds.

Pay very close attention to the insights revealed in the next three PRIMES. CORE PRIME, PARITY, and STAKE were some of the first PRIMES revealed to us over 30 years ago, and they are durable and applicable across a wide range of circumstances. They are also essential to driving meaningful outcomes in complex stakeholder environments.

I realized the importance of "intentionality" while visiting with my friend Dory Hollander, a psychologist and author. Dory had been my confidant and coach for many years and was in her last stage of battling cancer. I knew this would be the last time we talked, and so I asked her, "If you only had one chance, what advice would you give to a young person entering the business world today?" Dory smiled and said that she had the chance to ask her mentor that very question when he was dying and she could think of no better answer than the one he gave her. She said, "Be intentional. Persist variously."

Leadership in a learning organization starts with the principle of creative tension. Creative tension comes from seeing clearly where we want to be, our "vision," and telling the truth about where we are, our "current reality." The gap between the two generates a natural tension.

> Peter Senge[1]

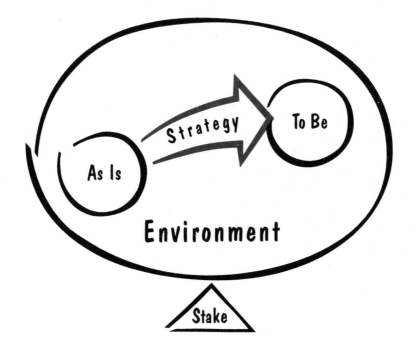

CORE PRIME

CORE PRIME

*How do you help the group to focus on the right things
and feel urgent about acting?*

When you need to enlist others to achieve your outcome, you must employ the essential skill of enrollment to take people beyond mere compliance. They must be inspired by the possibilities of your vision, committed to the outcomes, and willing to act unreasonably, if necessary, to achieve them. Enrollment results in a felt creative tension among stakeholders. They know where they are, where they are going, and why the journey is important.

The CORE PRIME distinguishes five essential agreements that generate creative tension and establish deep and sustainable shared intent:

1. **As Is**—Stakeholders must see their current situation—the whole thing—as it really is as opposed to how they want it to be.

2. **Environment**—They must agree on what's happening around them—which they're unable to affect but which will affect them.

3. **Stake**—They must agree on what's at stake if they stay where they are and don't change.

4. **To Be**—They must agree on a vision of the future with which they have fallen in love.

5. **Strategy**—Finally, they must agree on how to break out of the "As Is" and chart a course toward the "To Be."

The CORE PRIME is where everything begins and ends. It's immutable, and there's no room for interpretation. If you remove one of the five agreements, the whole thing falls apart. Not only is the CORE PRIME inflexible, it is often violated, and there's no learning curve. Get it right, you pass. Get it wrong, you fail.

The following are five agreements you must forge with your group in order to implement the CORE PRIME. Ask yourself as you take in each one, "Doesn't this just make perfect sense?"

Only by acceptance of the past can you alter it.

          ❧ T. S. Eliot[2]

AGREEMENT #1: AS IS

What you resist persists. What you embrace disappears.

Before anyone will go along with you, he or she must believe in you. Your ability to accept things as they actually are (as opposed to how you would like them to be) is how you gain credibility as a leader. Proof that you understand the current reality lies in your capacity to say, "This is how things are now," and for others to respond, "Yeah, that's how the situation looks to me as well."

Consider the rule stated above: "What you resist persists. What you embrace loses all its power over you." So name and embrace it all: the good, the bad, and the ugly. People may listen politely if you try to "spin" what's truly going on, but they'll walk away as soon as they can. People don't trust leaders who demonstrate a lack of appreciation for reality and who can't honestly acknowledge the way things really are. The "As Is" conversation is descriptive and fact based. You must set aside judgment and blame, thereby clearing the way for people to offer their perspective without fear.

It seems like common sense to state the obvious thrust of the "As Is"; however, it's something most leaders either fail to do authentically or altogether. Demonstrating a deep comprehension of the world as it is creates the foundation for everything that follows. Eventually, the group will establish a collective sense of the "As Is." Gaining this agreement can be the most difficult part of the CORE PRIME.

AGREEMENT #2: ENVIRONMENT

Recognize and leverage the uncontrollable.

This conversation identifies outside forces that can move you forward or hold you back. These are the forces that surround you but over which you have no control. An example of this kind of force is the economy. Most people would agree that nothing they do affects the economy directly. Auto mechanics may see a bad economy as a driving force for people to hold on to their older cars longer. Real estate developers may see the same bad economy as being a damper on new home sales.

In the illustration of the CORE PRIME, the "As Is," the "To Be," and the "Strategy" float within the "Environment." In this situation, the group must have a shared sense of what environmental forces are affecting or will affect them. Major trends in employment, the cost of energy, interest rates, and housing costs are examples of environmental forces that most people cannot control. But what the group needs to care about are the ones that will impact them in a significant way.

Recognizing what is beyond your control doesn't mean ignoring it. That would be like choosing to climb a mountain and disregarding the weather. You've gone to the trouble of packing the best gear and mustering all your determination and commitment; you aren't about to blow off the weather reports. While you may not be able to control the weather, it has the potential to exert enormous control over you—so much so that ignoring it might mean putting your life at risk.

The underlying question is, "Do you want to fight the 'Environment,' or do you want to ride it?" Pay attention to forces beyond your control and they'll carry you places you couldn't reach on your own. Ignore them and you may never know what hit you.

AGREEMENT #3: THE STAKE

Foster the most important agreement!

The "Stake" conversation represents "the fulcrum of possibility." Get it right and people tip toward the "To Be." Get it wrong, or under-invest in it, and people tip back to what is familiar. They'll guard the status quo as if their lives depended on it. The "Stake" conversation answers the question "What happens if we fail to drive toward the 'To Be' and remain where we are, doing what we're doing?"

How many strategic plans end up gathering dust on bookshelves? How many times will a friend complain about his weight, pledge to get in shape, but never do it? How many targeted reductions in greenhouse gases will we fail to achieve? Regardless of how much we complain about the "As Is," and no matter how inspired we are by our "To Be," nothing will happen until something we deem sufficiently significant is at risk.

A powerful "Stake" makes the status quo seem more dangerous than a leap into the unknown future. The "Stake" is at the heart of any effort to solve a problem, effect a change, or transform a system. Success literally rests on the "Stake."

Over the next few chapters, we'll answer the question, "What's at stake?" You'll need the answers, not just to avoid negative consequences but to let go of the status quo. Failing to do so will cause you to miss the experience of achieving your vision.

AGREEMENT #4: TO BE

Re-invent the future.

Vision creates the context for every endeavor and every goal. This conversation compels people to stand taller and speak with more deliberation; they grow confident, experience insight, and gain perspective. The "To Be" creates a reverence like that which many people felt when they heard Martin Luther King Jr. declare, "I have a dream." Every great leader is called to share a vision with which others literally fall in love. You don't create this vision alone, nor should you, even if you could.

We've already seen that the greatest visions are always DYNAMICALLY INCOMPLETE—always emerging. They are never fully detailed, as the voids are what invite others to cocreate.

The first four agreements establish a collective creative tension. We agree on where we are (As Is), where we are going (To Be), and why it is important to get there (Stake). We understand the forces that can propel us or restrain us (Environment). Only now is the group ready, willing, and able to build a strategy.

AGREEMENT #5: STRATEGY

Focus everything on what you want.

You've presented your vision and enrolled others in the quest. Your word—your INTEGRITY—depends on determining the "Strategy": who does what and when. The notion of "strategic planning" often brings up negative connotations because too many people engage in this process without precision. After years of trial and error, we uncovered the essential principles of building and implementing a powerful strategy.

The CORE PRIME shows that an effective strategy rescues people from their current state and propels them into a compelling future, because the stakes are so high.

When you can develop and present a strategy, you can transform anxiety over the gap between the past and the future into purposeful activity. However, this only happens when you focus on the fewest, most essential things that will alter the "As Is." If your strategy is insufficient to bring order to the energy created by change, chaos ensues—and your process will spin out of control.

The "Strategy" resolves the intense creative tension between authentically embracing the "As Is"—which the "Stake" revealed to be dangerous—and the ennobling vision of the "To Be." There can be no "strategies," as this word should never be made plural. You must use only one strategy at any given time to resolve the tension between what you have and what you want. Its job is to illuminate what actions you must take to realize your vision.

Rigor alone is paralytic death, imagination alone is insanity.

❧ Gregory Bateson[3]

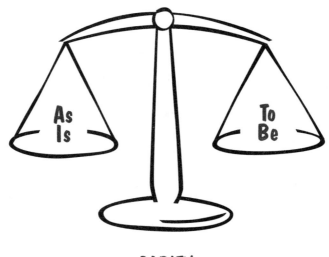

PARITY

PARITY

What is the right ratio of analyzing versus imagining?

The CORE PRIME revealed what conversations must happen to enroll others to drive change and cause transformation. The PARITY PRIME reveals how to have those conversations.

PARITY means devoting equal attention and detail to each of the five conversations in the CORE PRIME. It would be unwise and unhelpful to overanalyze the "As Is" and immediately attempt to build a high-level vision. Additionally, to focus on the "As Is" and the "To Be" while you give only lip service to the "Strategy" and the "Stake" is equally shortsighted. PARITY contributes to your success by ensuring that you pay the right amount of attention to each of the five components of the CORE PRIME.

I have noticed over the years that groups tend to focus on one or two of the elements of the CORE PRIME more so than others. Here are the types of groups:

ANALYSIS PARALYSIS

Analysis Paralysis groups are most comfortable talking—or arguing—about the current situation, without ever discussing what's at stake if they don't change. They are excessively introspective, are often uncomfortable with the idea of creating a vision, and may even feel they have no right to do so. To an outsider, these groups may sound like victims.

BLUE SKY

This term describes groups that are most comfortable when they dream about the future. Their characteristics are the opposite of those of Analysis Paralysis, as Blue Sky groups find the status quo tedious and even embarrassing to discuss. They assume they understand the "Stake" when in fact they often don't. Unfortunately, their lack of attention to the "As Is" causes them to be ungrounded. They seem to lack credibility and a secure sense of reality. Typically, the visions they develop fail to inspire people, including themselves.

BLUR

This kind of group is neither comfortable nor patient enough to drive agreement on the "As Is," the "To Be," or the "Stake." They're made up of Type A personalities and have an almost intractable bias toward action. Members of Blur groups only want to perform "real work." Without agreement on the beginning and the end, however, their efforts are usually unfocused, inefficient, and ineffective.

BALANCE

A balanced group is willing to go slow to go fast. Members take time to forge deep and comprehensive agreements between the stakeholders across each element of the CORE PRIME. They adhere to the "cruel rule of reciprocity," which states that agreement on the "As Is" will elicit deep understanding of an inspiring "To Be," and a deeply felt "Stake" will provide the impetus to take action. A detailed and cogent strategy is all that remains to organize the activity.

PARITY is more than a guideline. Like the CORE PRIME, you violate this principle at your peril.

There are three conversions a person needs to experience: the conversion of the head; the conversion of the heart; and the conversion of the pocketbook.

ॐ Martin Luther[4]

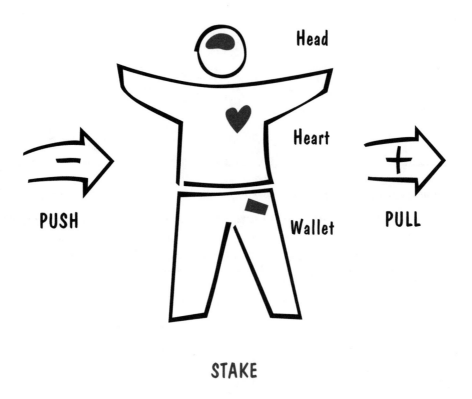

PUSH

PULL

Head

Heart

Wallet

STAKE

STAKE

How do you get the group "all in"?

The illustration of the CORE PRIME included a small triangle at the bottom titled STAKE, which fuels any effort to solve a problem, effect a change, or transform a system. Success literally rests on the STAKE, as it serves as the fulcrum of possibility. Organizations often call me in when change efforts are lagging or failing—and the very first thing I assess is whether the STAKE is clear to everybody. Frankly, I usually do not even have to look; I know immediately that the STAKE is not clear in a lagging change effort. If it were, the system would be changing. It is that simple.

People love to talk about radical changes in their lifestyles and how they're going to achieve those changes. They might claim that they're going to give up cigarettes and start an exercise routine, for example. Usually, you'll find them still talking and smoking the next day. We humans don't change very easily unless something we cherish is at stake. For the STAKE to be powerful enough to shatter the status quo, we have to believe that to remain in our current state is more dangerous than to embark on a risky journey that leads to an unknown future. As powerful as it may be, vision alone isn't enough.

After you've enlisted others in your transformation effort, some perfectly reasonable questions and doubts will arise among the same people who heeded your call and pledged their support. Even before they reach their offices, they recoil from the implications of their newly made agreement and wonder, "What role will I play?" They contemplate everything—from what they'll be asked to do to where their desks will be.

Before any change or transformation can occur, people must be convinced. The STAKE must therefore operate on organizational, community, and personal levels. This is why we closely examine our powerful STAKE conversation to dissect the patterns it reveals. From those revelations, we make the case for change.

The STAKE PRIME reminds us to make a comprehensive "case for change" by appealing to the following:

- Analytical people who listen with their brains.

- Emotional people who listen with their hearts.

- Financially motivated people who listen with their wallets.

When you're involved in a significant project that requires the enrollment of a large group, there will be a mix of all three types of people. Incentives are personal and often unique to each individual. There is no "one size fits all" when it comes to making the stake clear and establishing incentives for members of a group. You must therefore address each of their unique ways of listening.

Conversations about the STAKE lead most people to move quickly to avoid or push away from pain: "If we don't change, something bad is going to happen to us!" People will also pull toward experiences of pleasure: "If we realize our vision, look at all the good we can do/money we can make!" Powerful STAKE conversations must highlight both the detrimental aspects (what to avoid) and positive aspects (what people desire and want to pull toward them).

STAKE reveals six components of a robust answer to the question "What's at stake?" When you make the case for your vision, you must speak to the Head, Heart, and Wallet and address the negative results of staying put as well as the benefits of moving ahead.

During the financial meltdown in the first decade of the new millennium, local food banks knew that demand for their services was escalating beyond their capacity (push–Head). More and more people were going hungry as a result (push–Heart). Donations were down (push–Wallet). At the same time, they envisioned new partnerships with restaurants and grocery stores to eliminate waste by making better food available in greater quantities (pull–Head). They further imagined a transformation of their organizational purpose—from one of food distribution for sustenance to one of wellness nutrition services (pull–Heart)—all conducted in a cost-effective fashion (pull–Wallet).

Almost everyone present at planning meetings will complain about the status quo. They'll engage in deep conversation about solving problems and causing transformational outcomes. They will wave the flag and sing the rally song. But unless someone makes a powerfully rational, heartfelt, and financially compelling case for change, they'll go back to what they know—and will continue to complain about how things should be different.

Consider all six aspects illustrated in the STAKE PRIME: Head, Heart, and Wallet as well as their corresponding pushes/pulls. You will dramatically improve your chances of persuading people to embrace the vision and free themselves from the grip of the status quo as you make the case for transformation.

The STAKE works at organizational and individual levels. You must therefore embark on the journey only when each member of the team has a clear understanding of what is personally at stake for them.

Everyone who achieves success in a great venture solved each problem as they came to it. They helped themselves. And they were helped through powers known and unknown to them at the time they set out on their voyage. They kept going regardless of the obstacles they met.

                                                    W. C. Stone[5]

CHAPTER 6

TAKING COORDINATED ACTION

How do you get the group to do everything persistently about a few
critical things versus doing a few things about everything?

I raised six kids in the Washington, DC, area and got to watch a fair amount of soccer from elementary through high school. Initially, the kids all ran to the ball in a clump. Invariably, over time, as roles became clear and discipline became a shared value, I watched the most beautiful game emerge from the chaos. The key to this heightened performance was the overall coordination of individuals' actions.

Mastering the three PRIMES revealed in Chapter 6 will allow you to help your groups achieve this same level of performance and coordination. First and foremost, you will ensure that the group agrees fully about the point from which it is starting, where it is going, and how it is going to get there. Second, you will understand how to organize the effort to ensure that everything happens as it should and how to deal with surprises quickly when they arise. Finally, you will be equipped to recognize and minimize any energy the group is wasting on non-value-added activity.

Coordinated action represents the third and final corner of the POWER PRIME. The other two corners—shared perspective and shared intent—are essential but worthless if the group fails to act and produce real and intended outcomes. You create lasting value in coordinated action.

Cohesion, n.

1. The act of sticking together.

     ❧ American Dictionary of the English Language, Noah Webster, 1877

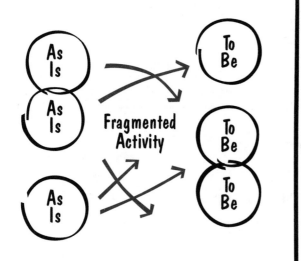

COHESION

COHESION

*Cohesion is an unnatural state for a group. How good
are you at establishing and sustaining it?*

COHESION may be one of the most critical elements to manage as a group charges against its challenges. It is present when everyone gives the same answers to the following three questions:

1. Where are we starting?

2. Where are we going?

3. What do we have to do to get there?

COHESION among group members is an unnatural state that requires constant energy to maintain. Without the group's investment in it, individuals tend to have slightly—or significantly—different views of their current situation, the urgency to change, and where they are headed. While this is natural, these differences—when unchecked—fragment the group's focus, dissipate its energy, and create an environment ripe for conflict. The COHESION PRIME reminds us that people work on different activities for different reasons and at different intensities. So expect fragmentation, but invest to establish and maintain COHESION.

---

*Success is focusing the full power of all you are on what you have a burning
desire to achieve.*

                    ❧ Wilfred Peterson[1]

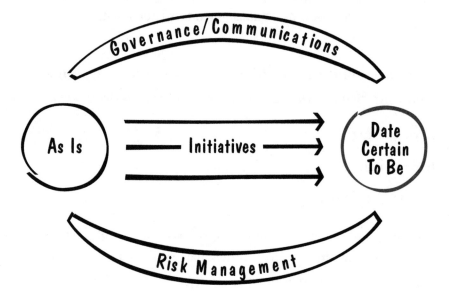

REDPOINT

REDPOINT

A good question to ask is, "What is important to do?" A better
question is, "Of all the important things we could do,
what are the fewest, most important?"

In the mid-1970s, German rock-climbing legend Kurt Albert painted red marks at the bases of routes he became skilled enough to climb without using any supports or aids other than his hands, feet, and limbs. In many ways, Albert's REDPOINT system was the origin of the free-climbing movement that led to the development of sport climbing a decade later. For our purposes, the term REDPOINT refers to a path that is marked for leaders and teams to overcome challenges, attain their visions, and dent the universe.

The REDPOINT PRIME can be summed up in one word: focus. It reveals the fastest, least risky path from our "As Is" to our "To Be." At its core, REDPOINT embodies a simple concept: Rather than do a few things about everything, the most powerful leaders and teams do everything about the fewest, most important things. They willingly live with complete INTEGRITY to realize their declared "To Be" on time.

Recall that the CORE PRIME makes the need clear to go from the "As Is" to the "To Be" because something important is at stake. Creative tension exists as a call to action. The Strategy arrow represents actions that will move a team from the "As Is" toward the possibilities of the "To Be." REDPOINT reveals how to make that journey.

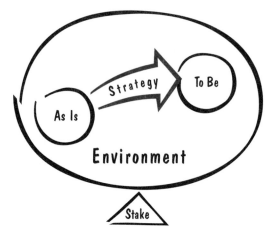

Before we examine the insights of the REDPOINT PRIME, it's important to understand the dangers inherent in the journey from the "As Is" to the "To Be." The US government has spent billions of dollars trying to modernize FAA air traffic systems, the Social Security Administration, the IRS tax administration process, the tax code, and government logistics. For a decade, it has tried to integrate enterprise resource management systems into the day-to-day management processes of the federal government. The Government Accountability Office reported in 2009 that the Federal Bureau of Investigation abandoned its "Virtual Case File" system after spending four years and $170 million to make it work. At the same time, the Department of Veterans Affairs abandoned its efforts to implement a patient appointment schedule system after spending eight years and $167 million. All of these projects have failed outright or come up short of expectations.[2]

There are dozens more examples like these, and the results are not restricted to government. The numbers from private industry are just as shocking. Various sources document an approximate failure rate of 70 percent for information technology (IT) projects. One study found that as many as 50 percent of all IT projects are considered "runaways," meaning they fit any two of the following three descriptions:

1.   More than 180 percent of the targeted time was required to complete a project.

2.   More than 160 percent of the estimated budget was consumed.

3.   Less than 70 percent of the targeted functionality was delivered.

The carnage extends beyond technology. Statistics show a failure rate of between 40 percent and 80 percent for most mergers and acquisitions. When defined in terms of shareholder value, the failure rate is 83 percent.[3]

The PRIMES you're outfitted with thus far enable you to avoid many of the mistakes that result in disasters like those cited.

The REDPOINT PRIME is made up of six elements, two of which are also found in the CORE PRIME: "As Is" and "To Be." Let's examine the other four elements.

INITIATIVES

Initiatives are projects with objectives, start times, milestones, and specific finish times. Assignment of the most effective initiatives to a REDPOINT requires us to ask penetrating questions. Rather than ask, for example, "What are the important things we need to do to reach our goal?" seasoned Universe Denters ask, "Of all the important things we need to do to leave the 'As Is' and move toward our 'To Be,' what are the fewest, most important things (one to three) that we must accomplish in the next 6, 12, or 18 months?"

The latter question forces ruthless prioritization and compels us to pay careful attention to time frames. Regardless of how long we must work to achieve our "To Be," it's critical to set interim REDPOINTS that can be achieved in six months and not more than 18 months; longer than that and focus is lost. Each REDPOINT should be designed so that its accomplishment is a cause for celebration.

Initiatives should have leaders, called "Lane Drivers." In large projects, "Portfolio Managers" may be assigned as resources for Lane Drivers and to coordinate their interaction and interdependence.

In the REDPOINT illustration, Initiatives are wrapped within a framework of three more elements: Governance, Communications, and Risk Management.

GOVERNANCE

Those who have the most power and resources and the most to lose must be ready to use overwhelming influence to resolve problems quickly, which people in the "lanes" may not be able or equipped to handle.

COMMUNICATIONS

Those responsible for developing and sharing the narrative or story about what's going on must do so in a manner that maintains maximum commitment, power, and momentum—yet eliminates resistance.

RISK MANAGEMENT

Those who look forward anticipate risks and intervene proactively to mitigate threats to schedules, quality, and costs.

REDPOINT is unique in six ways that are distinct from the principles that organizations typically use to implement most strategic initiatives—because it asks the following questions:

1. Who Helps Whom?

    Leadership teams usually delegate the implementation of strategic initiatives. Leaders often feel it's enough to see status reports and to "be available" to help implementation teams, should the need arise. This approach rarely works. REDPOINT implementation teams hold themselves directly accountable for success while everyone else—including their leaders—helps them. Vigilance is required to maintain this orientation.

The REDPOINT PRIME is virtually guaranteed to work when leaders take proactive measures with authority and commitment to date-certain outcomes to clear roadblocks from the path of transformation initiatives.

2. Who Uses Overwhelming Power?

In typical problem-solving and change efforts, governance teams (when they exist at all) meet at regular intervals and spend most of their time trying to reach a common starting point. REDPOINT governance teams convene only when problems arise and measure their success by how quickly they resolve them.

3. Who Needs Information as Oil?

Outside of REDPOINT, those responsible for communications are rarely held accountable for the amount of resistance to strategic initiatives or for establishing power through information sharing. Effective communication smooths the path for everyone and encourages understanding and acceptance of the changes that are happening.

4. What Is the Orientation?

"Scorekeepers" usually look backward and report on what has happened. REDPOINT scorekeepers look forward, anticipating what's ahead and finding ways to mitigate risk.

5. What Jeopardizes the Lock-On Date?

Deadlines don't budge in a project that recognizes the REDPOINT PRIME. When someone comes up with a new and valuable idea in other environments, the team extends the project deadline to accommodate it. When a new idea comes into a REDPOINT-based project, the first question asked is, "Can we do it and keep to our schedule?" If not, the idea is recorded and reserved for later consideration. When a deadline is in jeopardy, REDPOINT demands a decrease in scope that doesn't risk the value of the outcome. People become amazingly innovative when a leader takes this position.

Lock-On Date is the "incubator of innovation."

6.   When Is the End Near?

In a well-run, REDPOINT-based project, a sense of urgency helps teams maintain a fast operation tempo right from the start. When a natural lull occurs, every six months or so, it's time to acknowledge the team's efforts and make adjustments on the basis of what lies ahead.

For some leaders, the REDPOINT PRIME may provide a "shock of recognition"—when a PRIME jumps off the page, confirming what you have long felt was true but could never quite articulate. Perhaps you've worked on projects that didn't adhere to these principles. You know how that felt.

The REDPOINT PRIME tends to grow on you. The next time you're asked to join or lead a team, take another look at REDPOINT. If you're part of a team now, compare and contrast how yours is organized, and imagine how it might function if REDPOINT principles were introduced.

The next several PRIMES will reveal more deeply the insights contained in REDPOINT.

Most of what we say and do is not essential. If you can eliminate it, you'll have more time, and more tranquility. Ask yourself at every moment, "Is this necessary?"

           ❧ Marcus Aurelius, Meditations[4]

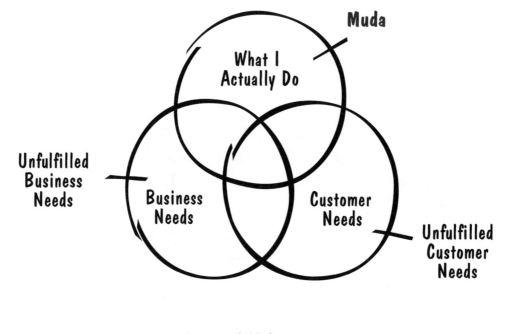

MUDA

MUDA

*Can you distinguish "non-value-added activity"? How much
of your group's resources is it consuming?*

MUDA is Japanese for "non-value added activity." MUDA happens when you are not paying attention. It builds up slowly, silently, and continuously until it chokes the system and contributes to a cloying sense of powerlessness. Meetings are a huge source of MUDA. In 2005 the US Bureau of Labor Statistics reported that unnecessary meetings cost US businesses approximately $37 billion each year.

Any time you are doing something, you are either adding value to your business, adding value to your customers, adding value to both, or wasting resources. The MUDA PRIME enables you to distinguish where you spend your time into 7 unique categories:

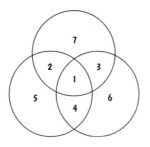

1.   This is where you are actually spending time doing things that address BOTH customers and business needs.

2.   This is where you are spending time taking care of strictly business needs.

3.   This is where you are spending time taking care of strictly customer needs.

4.   This area represents needs common to BOTH customers and the business that you are not addressing.

5.   This area represents business needs that you are not addressing.

6.   This area represents customer needs that you are not addressing.

7.   This area represents activities that you are spending your time on that do not address business or customer needs (MUDA).

MUDA is easier to identify when you are clear about the needs of your customers and business, the nearer you are to a deadline, or the fewer the resources available. It is harder to spot MUDA when you lack focus or have access to abundant resources.

Over the last four years, I have informally polled my clients to identify how many of the last 10 e-mails they received would be considered MUDA. The answers tightly range between 8 and 9. Roughly 80 percent of the time you spend dealing with e-mail is MUDA.

The MUDA PRIME illuminates a way to quickly and continuously ensure that all available resources are concentrated on the most important aspects of business and customer needs. If you are like me, your days are filled with "doing things." MUDA PRIME reveals a way to figure out if you are doing the right things. Once we recognize the fact, MUDA isn't hard to eliminate:

•   STOP spending time and money on non-value-added activities.

•   START investing freed-up time and money on unfulfilled business and customer needs.

Adventure is a path. Real adventure—self-determined, self-motivated, often risky—forces you to have firsthand encounters with the world. The world the way it is, not the way you imagine it. Your body will collide with the earth and you will bear witness. In this way you will be compelled to grapple with the limitless kindness and bottomless cruelty of humankind—and perhaps realize that you yourself are capable of both. This will change you. Nothing will ever again be black-and-white.

℘ Mark Jenkins[5]

PART 3

UNIVERSAL PATTERNS OF OUTSTANDING GROUP PERFORMANCE

What do high-performance groups know and do that low-performance groups do not?

The 18 PRIMES revealed so far outfit you to set yourself and the group up for success, generate power, and take initial action. This is essential but not sufficient to ensure your success. You and your group must proactively prepare yourselves to deal with quickly developing situations that require timely assessments and course corrections. The PRIMES you are about to uncover ensure that you can sustain the power and performance of the group through any unplanned developments until the outcomes you declared are fully realized.

First, you and your group must deal with things as they are, and have the capacity to make decisions as quickly as the situation demands. You will need to determine what behaviors you'll tolerate and not tolerate. Each and every group member must be comfortable making demands and requests of others and trust that they will keep agreements. Finally, the group must be skilled at and open to having fierce conversations and saying whatever needs to be said along the way to ensure success.

The PRIMES revealed in Part 3 are valuable life skills. People who attend PRIMES Training Workshops report that these have general applicability throughout all aspects of their business and personal lives.

CHAPTER 7

MAKING DECISIONS

What does the word "decision" actually mean? How are decisions made?

The act of making a decision is one of the most exciting and significant moments in a business and problem-solving context. In the context of the PRIMES, decisions are "irrevocable allocation of resources."

The group may have used brainstorming to generate ideas and get to "the end of what it knows" to get to this point. Members of the group might have taken the next step and formed various recommendations. However, the only way to cash in on the energy invested thus far is for someone to *make a decision*.

The truth is that a single individual makes a decision in a single moment. Contrary to some popular notions of leadership, groups do not make decisions.

Chapter 7 will introduce you to three PRIMES that will enable you to powerfully participate in the decision-making process. They'll describe how to select the most appropriate way to make decisions in a variety of circumstances. You will sharpen your skills in recognizing real decisions being made and in leading a group to a consensus.

The more you are willing to accept responsibility for your actions, the more credibility you will have.

❧ Brian Koslow[1]

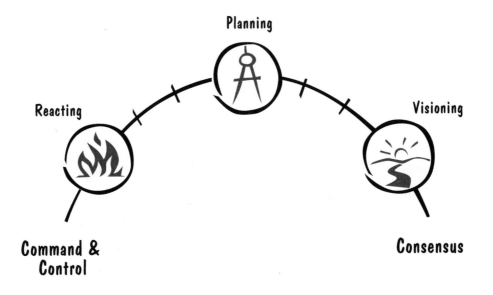

LEADERSHIP SPECTRUM

LEADERSHIP SPECTRUM

Are you the kind of leader who likes to facilitate consensus?
The right answer is, "That depends."

I've observed over the years that leaders tend to have a "default" style and a favorite decision-making process. Some are more comfortable making command-and-control decisions, while others prefer to collaborate with their subordinates and peers. The most effective leaders I've observed use the LEADERSHIP SPECTRUM PRIME and match the decision process to each situation.

The LEADERSHIP SPECTRUM PRIME was made crystal clear to me when I had the privilege of watching a Marine Corps general in the midst of criticizing his fellow officers for overusing the command-and-control decision process of combat. He drew the LEADERSHIP SPECTRUM on a flip chart and told his officers, "We cannot use command and control to develop our vision. When you guys were colonels getting ready to lead a charge on an enemy installment, the last thing your young Marines wanted to do was 'brainstorm' for the wisdom of the crowd. They needed you to issue orders with confidence and from deep experience. But we are not colonels. We are general officers at the headquarters of the US Marines Corps. We are preparing the USMC for the future. My expectation is that each and every day you will be moving across this spectrum. I want you to put four decision processes, from across this spectrum, in your pocket every morning. Get good at every one of them and get good at figuring out which one best fits each situation you encounter throughout the day."

Here are a few leadership styles:

- *Command and Control:* Use this leadership style when the situation is urgent and the stakes are high. Someone has to take command and control in the heat of battle.

- *Informed Command and Control:* This leadership style works well in situations that are still urgent but with lower stakes—such as when a company requires a meeting venue and reservations must be made within hours.

- *Limited Consensus:* Use this style for low-stakes strategic planning, such as making a choice between competing but similar health insurance plans.

- *Consensus:* Put this in your pocket for high-stakes strategic planning and visioning, such as creating a five-year plan to take a new company into the marketplace.

On one end of the LEADERSHIP SPECTRUM, Command and Control is preferred when time is short and any decision made fast is better than a perfect one made too late. People have trouble finding the right balance regarding this approach; they overuse or underuse it. It's best to use it for any type of emergency but also for smaller decisions where the marginal gain from collaboration is eclipsed by cost. It is hard for someone like myself who runs a consulting company to go two days without making command-and-control decisions.

Consensus is on the other end of the LEADERSHIP SPECTRUM. This process, as described in the CONSENSUS PRIME, is most appropriate for strategic planning and the exploration of innovations and breakthrough ideas. Ineffective leaders also overuse consensus decision making and rely on it even when situations cry out for rapid command-and-control decisions. Again, the root of this tendency is a fear of looking bad and taking responsibility.

Consensus decision processes work best if:

- Participants are given a deadline, and

- A backup decision process is clear from the start—one that will be used should the consensus process fail to result in a decision or agreement in the allotted time.

I can't give you a surefire formula for success, but I can give you a formula for failure: try to please everybody all the time.

❧ Herbert Bayard Swope[2]

---

1. ☑ The process was explicit, rational, and fair;

2. ☑ I was treated well and my inputs were heard;

3. ☑ I can live with and commit to the outcomes.

CONSENSUS

CONSENSUS

Are you still using the traditional definition of consensus?
Are you aware of how destructive the traditional definition is?

The most challenging environments in which to pursue transformation and problem solving are institutes of higher learning and multilateral organizations like the World Bank, the International Finance Corporation, and the United Nations. They're stuffed full with brilliant people. Yet as Peter Keen, a gifted colleague at the World Bank, once remarked, "Intelligence is like having four-wheel drive: you usually end up stuck like everybody else, just in a more remote location."

When I sat with Michael Doyle one afternoon and lamented my inability to secure a critical decision at the World Bank, he asked gently, "What are you trying to do?" I replied, "I'm just trying to get everyone to agree!" Michael looked at me penetratingly and said, "Why would you ever try to do that?" Then he took a napkin and drew the CONSENSUS PRIME. He called it a working definition of consensus and helped me see the group's lack of agreement in a new way. I immediately understood that my job was *not* to get everyone to agree. Setting this as my goal immediately gave any single rogue individual disproportionate power. A bad actor need only "disagree" (see LAGGARD PRIME) and consensus would be impossible.

My job, and your job, is to get the group to adopt the working definition of CONSENSUS embodied in this PRIME, then make sure that everyone answers "yes" to the following three questions:

1.   **Process Satisfaction:** Was the process we used explicit, rational, and fair?

2.   **Personal Treatment:** Were you, personally, treated well? Did you have ample opportunity to be heard, to make your opinions known, and to consider others' opinions?

3.   **Outcome Satisfaction:** Can you *live with* the outcome and commit to supporting the decisions of the group? (Notice the words *live with* as opposed to *agree with*. This is a critical distinction.)

Michael's point was that if people are satisfied with the first two elements, they typically agree to the third.

A word of caution: If people say "yes" to #3 but are dissatisfied with #1 and/or #2, their commitment is not likely to endure. Process satisfaction and personal treatment satisfaction are foundational parts of a person's commitment to support the group's outcomes.

I never leave home without the CONSENSUS PRIME.

There are more than 160 words in the dictionary that end in "-cide." Cide *derives from the Latin word for "kill."*

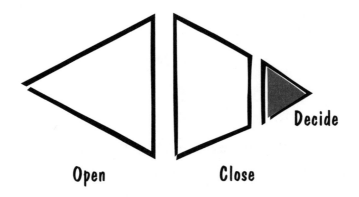

Open

Close

Decide

OPEN–CLOSE–DECIDE

OPEN–CLOSE–DECIDE

How do groups actually make decisions?

In the late 1980s, I got involved in IBM's development of what we called "group decision support systems" (GDSS). Though I had the money and technical capacity I needed, I lacked a true understanding of how groups made decisions. After conducting exhaustive research and discussing the matter with various psychologists and behaviorists, I found myself more confused than ever. Someone gave me a copy of Michael Doyle's book *How to Make Meetings Work*, which he coauthored with David Strauss. The book prompted me to reach out to Michael Doyle.[3]

Michael introduced me to Kai Dozier, and together they gave my group the insight we needed to develop our GDSS products: the OPEN–CLOSE–DECIDE PRIME. Once it had been revealed, I saw it everywhere, from boardrooms at J. P. Morgan to a group of friends trying to decide where to grab lunch. Whether the choice is a risky product launch or which dress to buy, OPEN–CLOSE–DECIDE is at work.

Michael and Kai explained that there is an initial period of time when groups tolerate the generation of ideas (OPEN). Brainstorming is an effective technique for structuring discussion during the OPEN phase. But the group eventually becomes less tolerant of new ideas and begins to prioritize and converge (CLOSE). Members of the group spend most of this phase arguing the merits of increasingly fewer choices. Finally, the group enters the third phase of the process, when a selection is made (DECIDE).

OPEN

The OPEN phase is the most fun and the easiest to lead and facilitate. The stakes are low and anything goes. As long as a leader suspends judgment (See SHAPE SHIFTER PRIME) and makes it safe for people to offer their opinions and ideas, they'll realize the primary value of the OPEN phase. Teams will generate fresh ideas and mash everything together to create innovative approaches. It is easy to build technology to support this "divergent" process. However, modern management gurus have exaggerated the importance of this part of the decision process. Any seasoned leader will tell you that generating ideas is the easy part; selecting and implementing the best ones is where the challenge lies.

CLOSE

Groups tend to enter the CLOSE phase when they run out of ideas, patience, or time. The stakes are higher than in the OPEN phase, and being right becomes more important than being provocative. The CLOSE phase is a convergent process marked by a distinct tone of judgment; certain ideas are deemed worthy, and others are cast aside. Leaders must listen closely because this is where the group begins to reveal its "decision criteria."

Decision criteria typically follow the word "because," as in, "I don't think this is a good idea because it costs too much." The person who voices this statement makes it clear that he or she perceives cost as a major criterion in making a decision.

Another person might say, "I think it's a good idea. Yes, it costs more, but I still like it because it produces so much customer value." This speaker introduced a second criterion—"customer value"—and, at the same time, elevated its importance over cost. If you pay close attention, you will then hear the group begin to place relative weighting on each criterion. Criteria are useful only when there are fewer than seven and when they are weighted by relative importance. Distinguishing between ideas and criterion is a critical skill to master through practice.

The CLOSE phase eventually runs its course naturally, or the group starts to run out of time. This is when things really get fascinating.

DECIDE

Like genocide, pesticide, and suicide, DECIDE is about death ("-cide"). The DECIDE phase is the final act of killing off alternatives and leaving one option alive. As I stated before, regardless of how many people are involved in the OPEN and CLOSE discussions, groups don't make decisions. Real decision-making comes down to one person who chooses for the group.

I've learned to recognize the "DECIDE moment" in literally hundreds of high-stakes meetings. Sometimes, it's barely perceptible, even to the trained eye. It happens in an instant, with a nod or a remark made by the one person everyone is watching. There is one person who has the power in any group, and the expectation of the others, to DECIDE for all once sufficient time and attention have been given to the OPEN and CLOSE phases.

The "decider" may or may not be the person called "leader." Oftentimes, the decider is the informal leader. Regardless, it is a single individual making the decision in a single and observable moment.

Note that the DECIDE phase is distinct from the CLOSE phase. CLOSE is a convergent process, but not one that allocates resources. In this context, a "decision" is an irrevocable allocation of resources—in that it cannot be undone. And the group will now invest time and/or money as a result of the decision. Great leaders live for these moments.

Holding a vote is the lone exception to the rule that one person ultimately decides. However, this represents the lowest form of decision making. When collaboration fails and leadership can't be trusted, people surrender their opinions and allow math to decide. Although voting is prevalent in politics, it's rarely the mechanism of choice elsewhere. The vote represents the failure of CONSENSUS; it's the process of last resort, and it's the least effective.

So far, Internet-based applications have made the OPEN phase more efficient and more accessible. We can now generate more ideas from more people faster. We can also rate and vote on these ideas using the network. But so far, no one has made any real progress, beyond voting tools, on figuring out how to facilitate the DECIDE process on the network.

Culture "is" .... always. You shape it, or it shapes you.

CHAPTER 8

BUILDING AN INTENTIONAL CULTURE

Quick—what does "culture" mean? There are consequences to using more than seven words to define culture.

Culture is the most powerful determinant of how a group behaves. It is the line drawn by a group that separates the behaviors they will tolerate from that which they will not. The group enforces adherence to this line. Authorities cannot mandate culture.

Culture always exists; it is built either passively or actively, by default or intentionally. Culture can be implicit—that is, conveyed through stories and actions—or explicit, captured in a document or other medium.

When culture fails to drive behaviors that are essential to the success of the group or organization, authorities develop, implement, and enforce rules, policies, and laws. Excessive rules, policies, and laws represent a failure of culture.

An intentionally designed, powerful, and generative culture is a precious asset for the group to appreciate, value, and defend. The next three PRIMES reveal to you how to design and sustain an intentional culture that brings joy and high performance to your groups.

A culture is made—or destroyed—by its articulate voices.

இ Ayn Rand[1]

**Behaviors
We Tolerate**

—— **Culture** ——

**Behaviors
We Do Not
Tolerate**

CULTURE

CULTURE

Culture happens. You shape it or it shapes you.
How good are you at shaping a culture?

As stated previously, CULTURE represents the difference between the behaviors that groups tolerate—and encourage—and those that they do not tolerate.

Some groups make their culture explicit by writing it down. Stating the culture explicitly makes it easy for all, especially new members, to know where this line is. Explicit statements of culture also make it easier to reinforce and enforce the culture—especially for those lower in rank. This articulation is important because unlike with rules and policies, adherence to culture must be the responsibility of every member of the group regardless of placement in the hierarchy.

Rules and policies pale in comparison with CULTURE when it comes to determining behavior within any group. When a group steps up to state its culture on a piece of paper, its words literally create a place from which to stand and operate. These are some of the most senior conversations on the planet.

VALUES AND GUIDING PRINCIPLES—CULTURAL BUILDING BLOCKS

Values and Guiding Principles are essential building blocks of culture. However, it's frequently unclear what they are and how they are different from each other, yet intricately linked.

Values are single words that describe "ways of being." The group chooses to raise these words above all other words. These shared values make clear how the group members intend to seem to each other and those outside the group. It is best to limit yourself to three to seven stated values.

Throughout millennia and across the globe, communities have placed value on being honest, compassionate, respectful, responsible, and fair. In fact, these values are so consistent that they are now deemed "The Five Universal Values" (see Rushworth Kidder, *How Good People Make Tough Choices*). I suggest you consider these universal values as *givens* and focus instead on stating values that specifically apply to your group and are unique to what you are doing.

Guiding Principles are phrases that direct behavior. The essence of a Guiding Principle is a verb and a noun. For example, "Be interested first, then be interesting" directs a behavior. The following table makes clear the differences between Values and Guiding Principles.

Values	Guiding Principles
Single words	Short phrases
Abstract—invites discussion	Specific
Describes "How to be"	Describes "What to do"
Emphasizes the noun	Emphasizes the verb

Values and Guiding Principles are the essential building blocks of a Statement of Culture. The following are some best practices of those who are choosing to make their culture explicit by building a Statement of Culture:

- Understand that your culture *always* exists. You have a choice to write down what is or write down what you want. Be intentional.

- If you are going to write it down, make sure you make it easy for the group to give *feedback* to each other within the bounds of the cultural statement.

- Keep it simple. Not simplistic—*simple*. This is not as easy as it sounds.

- Make sure the top boss is committed. If he or she isn't willing to live the stated culture, do not state the culture.

- Make the culture clear in recruitment. These folks need to know what they are getting into.

- Make the culture clear in new employee orientation. These folks need to know what they are involved with.

- Make the culture clear to customers. Enrolling them will cause you to actually live into the statements you are making.

- Ask those leaving the group how the "experienced" culture matched up with the "stated" culture. These folks are in the best position to give you the real scoop.

- Publicly acknowledge those who stand for the culture.

- Be willing to change the Statement of Culture when you cannot get it to match the choices you are making on a daily basis. If you can't match it, make it match you.

Declaring your CULTURE explicitly can generate unprecedented power. There are risks, but they can be managed. Build your culture out of Values and Guiding Principles. Keep it simple. Declaring your culture explicitly and with INTEGRITY is one of the highest acts of creation available to mankind and ignites one of the most significant conversations on the planet. That conversation is, "How do we choose to be and behave?"

There are real benefits to declaring your culture explicitly; however, there are also two risks. First and foremost is the risk that some people will behave in an observable manner that is not congruent with the explicit stated culture and that no one will do anything about it. Enron had a Statement of Culture, behaved in a manner incongruent with that statement, and no one did anything about it. This breach of INTEGRITY eventually caused the failure of the company and the loss of wealth to thousands.

The second risk is that some individuals will use the Statement of Culture to hurt those they want to hurt. These people use Statements of Culture as rules of a club rather than as aspirations. They diminish their peers' power under the guise of "defender of culture."

The benefits of an explicit Statement of Culture far outweigh the risks, especially since the risks can be mitigated easily. The next two PRIMES are useful in ensuring that groups who choose to make their culture explicit generate unprecedented power with minimum risk. They are CONGRUENCE and FEEDBACK.

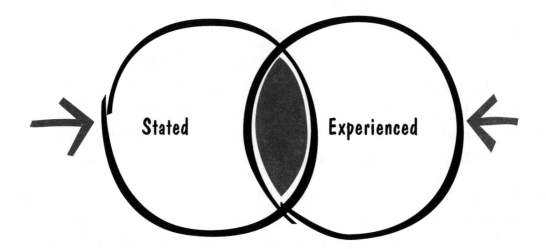

CONGRUENCE

CONGRUENCE

What is the dark side of a stated culture?

You now understand what CULTURE is and how to be intentional about the CULTURE in which you want to live. You realize that creating your intended CULTURE has benefits, including being easily reinforced at all levels of the organization. However, you are also aware that by stating your intended CULTURE, you run the risk of behaving in a way that is not congruent with what you've stated.

This risk is mitigated through the CONGRUENCE PRIME, which reveals the constant tension between what is "stated" and what is "experienced." In the illustration, the red arrows represent the continuous investment of energy that is required to ensure that the "stated" culture is the "experienced" culture.

Efforts to maintain CONGRUENCE must be authentic. On July 1, 2000, Ken Lay, Enron's Chairman and CEO, published the company's 62-page Code of Ethics and required everyone to sign it. The foreword to the document says:

> As officers and employees of Enron Corp., . . . we are responsible for conducting the business affairs of the company in accordance with all applicable laws and in a moral and honest manner. . . . We want to be proud of Enron and to know that it enjoys a reputation for fairness and honesty and that it is respected. Gaining such respect is one aim of our advertising and public relations activities,

but no matter how effective they may be, Enron's reputation finally depends on its people, on you and me. Let's keep that reputation high.

Lay got the second-to-last sentence right. That is about it. This whole thing talks about appearance (reputation). Notice how the statement reads that the company "enjoys a reputation for fairness and honesty" instead of "is fair and honest." Clearly, these individuals did not live in CONGRUENCE with this stated code. The system had no integrity—and people got hurt as a result.

A simple and fast way to determine how much CONGRUENCE your group is experiencing is to ask everyone to draw two circles, one labeled "stated" and another labeled "experienced," and ask them to overlap the circles to the degree they feel the stated culture is in fact the culture they are experiencing. Display all the papers and discuss what you see. Ask for specific stories about when the stated and experienced overlap and when they do not. This conversation will generate priceless insights about the group.

The energy that pushes these circles together is FEEDBACK. This occurs when someone says to someone else, "Hey, I want to acknowledge you for acting in congruence with our stated culture" (positive reinforcement) or "Hey, I don't think that what you are doing is congruent with our culture" (negative reinforcement). Of the two types of feedback, negative is the most powerful. The capacity and willingness of group members to give feedback to each other is essential to actually experiencing the culture that is stated.

To Speak or NOT to Speak

If it is not truthful and not helpful don't say it.

If it is truthful and not helpful don't say it.

If it is not truthful and helpful don't say it.

If it is both Truthful and Helpful . . . Wait for the

right time.

❧ Buddhist quote

✓ **Right Message**

✓ **Right Time**

✓ **Right Person**

✓ **Right Way**

✓ **Right Reason**

FEEDBACK AS CARING

FEEDBACK AS CARING

How good are you at giving it? How good are you at getting it?
Why does it matter?

High-performance groups see the giving of FEEDBACK as an outward expression of caring for someone. People who believe this about feedback understand the following concept: that how a person *thinks* he or she appears to others and how that person *actually* appears to others is often very different. The FEEDBACK AS CARING PRIME reveals how a person comes to see how others perceive him or her. The capacity to give and receive generative, effective, and timely feedback is essential to achieving powerful group performance.

FEEDBACK is the force that keeps the "experienced" culture aligned with the "stated" culture. FEEDBACK allows us to learn and grow because it is observable. As a consultant, I have immersed myself in dozens of companies over the past three decades. I have come to find that it is easy to determine which organizations have a healthy relationship to feedback and which ones do not. It did not take clients like Procter and Gamble, DuPont, The Four Seasons, and the Marine Corps very long to make it perfectly clear to me which behaviors they tolerate and which they don't. Yet their feedback was never too harsh; rather, it stemmed from the fact that they had pride in the culture they'd established and were extending an invitation to become part of it.

I have also gone into organizations feeling like there were unstated and undisclosed tripping hazards while getting the creepy sense that I may be making mistakes and not even knowing it. This feeling does not bring out my best, nor does it for most people in these circumstances.

I once worked with a long-standing law firm in the NYC area. After hearing me speak on the topic of "Building an Intentional Culture," the managing partner asked me to come in and work with the senior team on its culture. Larry Danner—who has a track record of designing, building, and leading highly effective schools—joined me on this project.[2] We interviewed a sample of the employees and quickly realized that the feedback channels were very convoluted. People talked about people to other people and were uncomfortable confronting each other when things were askew. Direct feedback was extremely limited. And people were not happy.

Larry first helped the top team see the value of effective FEEDBACK. Then he took a black marker and drew the FEEDBACK PRIME on a flip chart, conveying a simple message: Feedback is easy if the receiver sees it as an act of caring and if the giver takes the time to follow five basic guidelines:

1. *Craft the right message.* Take the time to consider what you are really trying to convey. How can you say it in a way that the receiver will really hear?

2. *Choose the right time.* Some people are morning people; others are night owls. Determine the best time for this particular receiver to get the message without distraction.

3. *Give it to the right person.* This might seem obvious. But it is essential to take time to consider who really needs the feedback.

4. *Deliver it in the right way.* Some people need a lot of context. Others prefer getting right to the point. The right way to deliver thefeedback is the way the receiver wants to get it. Each circumstance will be unique.

5. *Give feedback for the right reason.* Take the time to determine why you are giving this feedback. Is it for the benefit of the group or the receiver? Or is it for your own peace of mind? The best reason is usually a combination of all three. However, part of the reason *must* be because

you genuinely care for the person to whom you are giving the feedback and because you care for his or her future.

One last but critical point is that in this scenario, four out of five does not count. In other words, all five guidelines must be followed in order for FEEDBACK to be most effective.

Roots of the FEEDBACK AS CARING PRIME can be traced back to 350 BC in Aristotle's *Nicomachean Ethics*, where he states, "Anyone can become angry—that is easy. But to be angry with the right person, to the right degree, at the right time, for the right purpose, and in the right way—that is not easy."

Since that time when I worked with Larry, we have outfitted many groups with the FEEDBACK AS CARING PRIME as well as the other PRIMES revealed in this chapter. The good news is that they regularly create a profound and desired result.

I recently had a chance to work with a tech company in San Francisco that was experiencing extremely fast growth. Leadership did not want the regular arrival of new people to diffuse the culture that they felt allowed them to succeed. The team took to these PRIMES instantly and powerfully, and I can feel the difference in the air when I visit.

Don't be satisfied with a default culture or risk your fortunes on an implicit culture that can unknowingly shift and morph. Intentionally design a culture you love and one that drives performance. Ensure that group members experience the stated culture by creating an environment in which people see feedback as caring and deliver it with precision.

CHAPTER 9

SOCIAL CONTRACTING AND ACCOUNTABILITY WITHIN THE GROUP

How do peers give each other commands?

There are no unnecessary choke points in high-performance groups. Deals are getting cut laterally, up, and down as appropriate. Junior people are making requests of senior people. Peers are giving commands to each other. Work is being delegated in all directions. When it is working right, productivity is astonishing. You can witness a primitive occurrence of high-speed social contracting any day of the week by walking into any well-managed national fast food franchise at lunchtime. You will hear rapid-fire commands, scripted requests, and confirmations of agreements.

This level of performance is possible because of social contracting among group members. This process determines how work is delegated and tasks are assigned in situations in which people can't wait for a boss to get involved—or when there is no common boss.

Chapter 9 presents three PRIMES that greatly facilitate a group's ability to establish social contracts. These PRIMES will enable you to make communication equivalent to action. Talking will no longer *lead* to action; it will *be* action. You can redirect time spent "checking up on commitments and deadlines" to "driving outcomes."

Before jumping into this chapter, make sure you understand the INTEGRITY PRIME as it is revealed in Chapter 2. INTEGRITY is at the heart of social contracting.

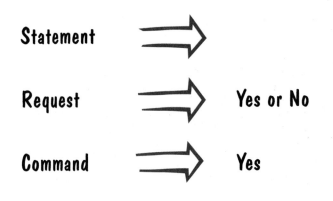

REQUEST–COMMAND

REQUEST

Why saying "no" protects your saying "yes."

Parties can forge powerful social contracts only when they recognize what they are doing. While that may seem like an obvious statement, I invite you, upon completion of reading this chapter, to observe how recklessly people enter into social contracts in your work environment. You will see passive statements cloaked as requests and people not even realizing that they are in fact giving their word.

Recognizing social contracts requires all members of the group to distinguish "statements" from "requests" from "commands." These are completely different concepts, and the differences are critical to recognize.

A "statement" is a description of something or the condition of someone. Examples are:

"Our profits are declining."

"The garbage needs to go out."

"I am so frustrated by what you did."

"I'm hungry."

"It would be nice if someone would give Joe a call."

"It would be great if you could get the report to me by tomorrow."

No response is required, and there is no opening to give your word.

A "request" is an invitation to give your word.[1] Requests sound like:

"Will you get me an analysis of why our profits are declining by tomorrow afternoon?"

"Will you please take the garbage out before you go to bed?"

"Will you let me explain why you frustrated me?"

"Will you make sure someone calls Joe today?"

"Will you get me the report by tomorrow?"

Notice how a REQUEST is an invitation for someone to give his or her word and how it requires a response. Only two responses to a REQUEST are allowed in high-performance groups: "no" and "yes." "Maybe" or "I'll try" are code words for "no," and their use should be forbidden.

A "command" is a requirement for someone to make good on his or her word. Commands sound like this:

"Get me the analysis of why our profits are declining by tomorrow afternoon."

"Take the garbage out before you go to bed."

"Sit down. I am going to tell you why I am frustrated."

"Please make me a ham sandwich."

"Call Joe today."

"Get me that report by tomorrow."

Commands are an essential part of high-performance social contracting, and the only response to them is "yes." Though not used often, they are the fastest way to get stuff done.

Too many people cloak requests as statements and requests as commands, which confuses and frustrates everybody. The following is a step-by-step process that will allow you to embed the capacity for effective and efficient social contracting into groups:

1. Make sure everybody can discern the difference between a statement, a request, and a command and recognize—in the moment—which is being said by them or to them.

2. Make sure everybody understands that statements do not require responses or actions.

3. Make sure that when a request is made of someone, that person has a right to say "no" without any repercussions. In fact, most responses to requests are "no" in cultures of integrity. People say "yes" only when they absolutely mean it, when integrity is a core, shared value. "No" is often a defender of previous "yes" promises. And precision matters in this business of integrity.

4. In the rare event that a command is required, the only possible response is "yes." However, it's appropriate to allow the person being commanded the opportunity to make the consequences of saying "yes" to the command clear to the one issuing the command. This sounds like, "Yes, Bill, I will have that report to you tomorrow but know that I will not be making the call on Joe as a result." It is important for the consequences of a command to be known to the one giving the command.

Distinguishing a REQUEST from a statement and a command is essential to effective social contracting—which in itself is essential to developing high-performance groups.

A single lie destroys a whole reputation of integrity.

જ Baltasar Gracian[2]

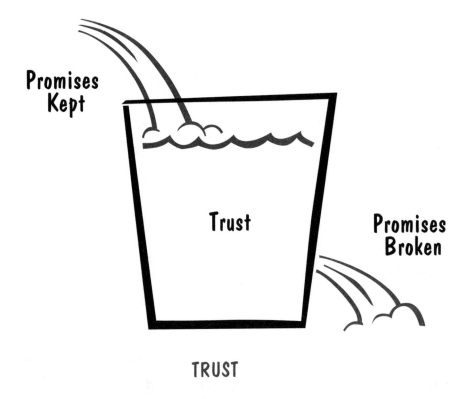

Promises Kept

Trust

Promises Broken

TRUST

TRUST

We all say how important trust is. What is trust?
How do you generate it and how do you destroy it?

Everyone discusses how critical it is for high-performance groups to establish trust. But what exactly is it? How do we generate—and destroy—TRUST? And if we do destroy it, can TRUST be regenerated?

To TRUST is to believe that a person keeps his or her word. That's it. Some people, upon first meeting, assume they can TRUST you. They start out relationships with a full TRUST bucket, while others start out with an empty bucket and need evidence to fill it. Frankly, this is a distinction without difference. It really does not matter how people choose to start out in relation to their TRUST in you because you have the power to generate TRUST. The key is to give your word and *keep it*—over and over again. Doing this will fill any trust bucket and/or keep it full.

Being trusted is the result of living in INTEGRITY with everyone you encounter. Every time someone makes a REQUEST of you, something is going to happen to the TRUST bucket.

This is why there are *no small requests*. Giving your word is giving your word regardless of the magnitude of the REQUEST. INTEGRITY is binary. You either keep your word or do not keep your word; size does not matter.

I have a friend who taught people how to be ambassadors in foreign countries. He introduced them to the concept of the "Three-fer" as a way to develop trust with skeptical strangers. As he explains to would-be ambassadors, "When you are new to a country, you must look for any small requests from the government officials you encounter. For example, let's say that a government official discovers you attended a particular university and has a daughter who is interested in applying there. So he asks if you could 'get her some information about the school'" (REQUEST).

In this scenario, my friend would advise the young ambassador not to give a course catalogue to the official, even if the ambassador happened to have one in his or her pocket—or else the ambassador would waste the opportunity for a "trust-building Three-fer." Instead, the ambassador should make a specific promise that sounds like, "Sir, I will bring the course catalogue to you this Friday at 9:30 AM." (PROMISE MADE). At exactly 9:30 AM on Friday, the ambassador would knock on the official's door and casually remind him or her of the promise made. It would sound like, "Sir, do you remember on Monday I told you I would bring you the course catalogue at 9:30 AM on Friday? Well, it is 9:30 AM on Friday, and here is the catalogue as promised" (REMINDER OF PROMISE MADE + PROMISE FULFILLED). The ambassador would then follow up three days later and say to the official, "I promised on Monday that I would bring you the catalogue on Friday at 9:30 AM, and I did that. I was wondering if your daughter might need anything else regarding the school" (REMINDER OF PROMISE MADE + REMINDER OF PROMISED FULFILLED).

"Your goal initially," my friend would instruct his students, "is to find seven seemingly trivial opportunities to give your word using the 'Three-fer Technique,' then negotiate peace."

A bucket full of trust shared between two or more people is a precious thing. It means we do not have to worry about things getting done or not getting done. Status reports become irrelevant. Synchronicity skyrockets. Keep your word on all matters large and small. Protect trusted relationships by being your word, always.

Forgiveness means giving up the right to punish someone.

❧ Father of one of the Amish children killed in the 2006
Nickel Mines School House massacre

SAY $\Longleftrightarrow$ DO

BREACH

BREACH

What do you do when your "yes" turns out to be a "no"?

The INTEGRITY, REQUEST, and TRUST PRIMES stress the criticality of being of your word. The BREACH PRIME reveals what to do when you do not keep your word.

For example, if you're late to a meeting after you committed to being on time, people will perceive your tardiness as a BREACH of INTEGRITY. Just as INTEGRITY fills the TRUST bucket, BREACH drains the TRUST bucket—and diminishes your POWER in the eyes of the group.

Despite a commitment and a willingness to maintain INTEGRITY, it's probable—perhaps even inevitable—that a BREACH will occur. When you realize that you have not been your word, you must clean things up quickly.

ACKNOWLEDGE AND RECOMMIT

Step 1: Acknowledge the BREACH

"I said I'd be here at nine o'clock, and I wasn't."

When someone acknowledges that he or she committed a BREACH, that person has taken the first step toward repair. If a person fails to acknowledge his or her BREACH, group members should point it out (see FEEDBACK). This is a way for the group to invite this person to reestablish his or her integrity and thus regain his or her power in the group. Taking a stand for someone's integrity is one of the highest acts of love and concern that group members can give each other.

Step 2: Recommit to **INTEGRITY**

"In the future, I'll be on time."

That's it. No excuses; they deflect accountability and waste more of the group's time.

If someone feels the need to apologize, he or she can do so between the first and second steps. It is unnecessary most of the time, however, since an apology is implied in the acknowledgment of a BREACH. More important than apologizing is asking for forgiveness.

When you REQUEST that someone forgive you for your BREACH of INTEGRITY, you are asking that person to give up his or her right to keep on punishing you for your BREACH. As with all REQUESTS, that person has the right to forgive you or not.

Rwandan President Paul Kagame once told me something profound about forgiveness that occurred when he was leading the country through a post-genocidal time of national reconciliation. He said that when a request is made for forgiveness and forgiveness is granted, the forgiver cannot ever discuss the BREACH again with the forgiven. This is not to say the matter is forgotten; it just couldn't be used against the one now forgiven.

The responsibility of the person who has BREACHED ends with the acknowledgement of the BREACH and the reestablishment of that person's commitment to be his or her word. The group can choose freely to forgive or not. That is out of the control of the person who BREACHED.

When outfitting groups with the BREACH PRIME, I am regularly asked what happens when someone commits to living in INTEGRITY but regularly BREACHES and cleans it up like nothing happened. Can someone abuse the BREACH PRIME? Though the short answer is "yes," that has not been my experience. INTEGRITY is a simple concept with profound implications. In my experience, I see people take it on with serious intent and sincerely clean up their BREACHES.

To recap what we've covered:

- High-performance groups are masters at social contracting.

- People establish social contracts by recognizing, making, and responding to REQUESTS.

- TRUST comes as a result of people always responding to REQUESTS with INTEGRITY.

- BREACH is when we fail to be our word.

- People can repair breaches by (1) acknowledging them without excuses, (2) recommitting to living in INTEGRITY with group, and (3) requesting forgiveness.

First, make sure the people around you declare to live in INTEGRITY with the other members of the group (or not). Next, teach them to distinguish statements, requests, and commands. And make sure "no" is an acceptable answer to requests.

Then make sure everybody has a picture in his or her mind of the trust bucket and is aware of the value of trust and how to generate it and sustain it. Finally, teach them how to clean up BREACHES of INTEGRITY and get over them. The rewards for following this plan are breathtaking.

CHAPTER 10

SAYING AND NOT SAYING; LISTENING AND NOT LISTENING

How do high-performance groups sound?

Members of high-performance groups are fearless when it comes to speaking their truths and they are eager to hear each other's truths. Indeed, their frankness can be unnerving to those who have not been indoctrinated.

People in high-performance groups are active listeners and distinguish facts from stories from beliefs in real time. They understand the importance of sharing their own beliefs and knowing those of others.

Finally, high-performance groups do not tolerate any form of gossip. They understand gossip's destructive nature, know how to recognize it, and have tools to stop it when it shows up.

The time it will take you to read this chapter will be long enough to master the three PRIMES it contains. There is no learning curve for these PRIMES; they provide value to the entire group, even if you are the only member of the group that applies them. Your unilateral application of these PRIMES the very next time you interact with the group will drive higher group performance.

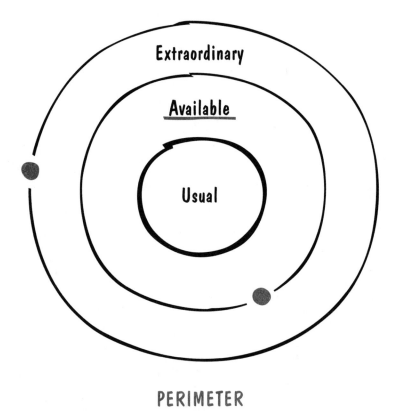

PERIMETER

PERIMETER

How small a fence have you built around what can and cannot be said?

The next time you are in a group, look around. See the fence? It encircles you and the group and separates what you and other members are willing to say to each other—and what you are not. Technically, this fence is called a "normative boundary." You may not be able to see it, but you can feel its presence. Whenever you are together with one or more people, a fence always exists. And whether you realize it or not, it limits the conversation.

Inside the fence is the "usual" conversation that generates the usual results. Outside the fence is the "available" conversation. Talking about things outside the fence is "unusual" and therefore generates remarkable outcomes.

The PERIMERTER PRIME first showed up when I was in New York working with a group of CEOs who asked me to outfit them with the PRIMES. Without much thought, I went to the butcher paper, drew the three circles, and said to them, "As we do introductions, tell me something about your business that you have never told any other member. Then I will ask the group to tell me how far out from 'usual' your comment was, so I get a gauge on the group." I knew 10 minutes later that a new PRIME was born. These seasoned executives were immediately able to take their conversation to a whole new level.

Try this. Start talking with someone you know as you usually do. Then tell or ask that person something you never did before. Make it something that you would like to share or know but you never found the right time or right circumstances in which to bring it up. This will allow you to genuinely exist in the available conversation space.

Problems persist in groups because of excessively tight perimeters that limit the problem solvers' conversation space. By using the PERIMETER PRIME, you can open up all the space the essential conversation needs by doing the following:

- USUAL:
  Draw a circle in the middle of the page and write "Usual" in the center.

  Say, "This is how we usually talk to each other in these meetings. We can say all the stuff in the middle of the circle, but we do not say any of the stuff outside of it. Therefore, we have created this fence."

- AVAILABLE:
  Draw a dashed line circle around the first circle. Label the space it makes "Available."

  Say, "We can move the fence out to give ourselves permission to discuss matters relevant to what we are doing but that we have not yet said. This will open up space for a bigger conversation."

- EXTRAORDINARY:
  Draw a dotted line circle out one more level and label its space "Extraordinary."

  Say, "We can even move our fence out farther. To create extraordinary outcomes, we need to have an extraordinary conversation."

- RED DOTS:
  Draw a big red dot in the "Available" space.

  Say, "For example, I think . . . ." Share something useful to the group's project that, for whatever reason, neither you nor anyone else has ever said. Then say, "And here is another 'red dot.'" Draw another red dot in the "Available" or even the "Extraordinary" space and say something that has not been said. You have led the group outside its normal perimeter of acceptable conversation. Now make a REQUEST. Ask people to join you out here in the "Available" or even "Extraordinary" space.

Once the fence has been distinguished, everybody sees and feels it. Eventually, someone will say, "I have a red dot." Then that person will discuss something he or she feels significantly adds to the conversation. After this, people will contribute red dot comments regularly, allowing entirely new insights to emerge.

The PERIMETER PRIME is easy to introduce to the group and has an instant and lasting effect. There is so much out there in the unsaid realm. Give PERIMETER a test drive the very next time you are working in a group.

He uses statistics as a drunken man uses lamp posts—for support rather than illumination.

        ❧ Andrew Lang[1]

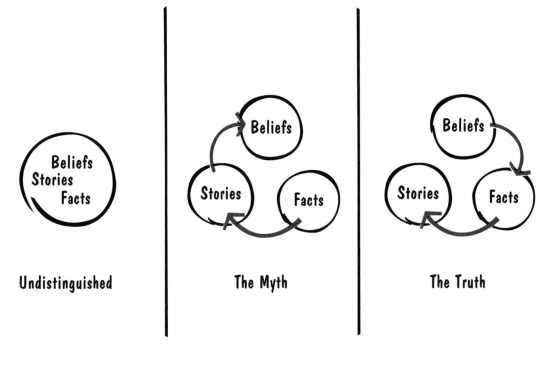

FACTS, STORIES, AND BELIEFS

FACTS, STORIES, AND BELIEFS

*Can you distinguish facts from stories from beliefs? Do you use facts the way
a drunk uses a lamp post—for support versus illumination?*

Facts, stories, and beliefs are not the same things. However, we fail to distinguish one from the other when engaged in discussions. Rightly parsing facts from stories from beliefs matters to leaders, change agents, and those who desire to dent the universe. Just as wars are fought by soldiers but caused by conflicting politicians, arguments are fought using facts but are caused by conflicting yet undistinguished beliefs. If you want to forge extraordinary agreements, facilitate resolutions to problems, and end persistent complaints, you must elevate the rhetoric away from a clash of facts and beyond time-wasting stories and get people to reveal their beliefs and the rationales behind them. Once they do so—and want to understand others' beliefs as well—a new level of learning and collaboration becomes available.

Consider the following two sentences:

"Our revenue was $50 million last year, and that is simply not enough. Marketing is inept."

Many listeners give each phrase equal treatment. People who fail to distinguish facts from stories from beliefs are represented on the left side of the FACTS, STORIES, AND BELIEFS PRIME; you can think of them as "passive listeners." These people cannot or do not recognize that the two sentences contain three distinct elements.

The next group of listeners, represented in the center of the PRIME, can distinguish facts from stories from beliefs. They see this:

"Our revenue was $50 million last year (FACT), and that is simply not enough (STORY). Marketing is inept (BELIEF)."

However, people in this group are living the "Joe Friday" myth. Lead detective Joe Friday from the TV show *Dragnet* would always say, "Just the facts, ma'am," when questioning a witness. Joe would piece together a story from these facts to explain the crime and help him find the guilty party. Such formulaic deductions may serve us well on TV and in controlled scientific experiments; however, we see a different progression at work in complex problem solving and transformation.

I call the third group, represented by the right side of this PRIME, the "Rightly Parsers." Like their Joe Friday colleagues, the Rightly Parsers actively distinguish each comment they hear as a fact, a story, or a belief. However, Rightly Parsers do not buy into the Joe Friday myth. They understand that every day, people wake up in the morning and put on their beliefs just like they put on their socks. Then they go out into the world and shop among all the facts for the select facts that back up their beliefs. They ignore facts that run counter to their beliefs. They then use these carefully selected facts to tell the stories that justify the beliefs they carried into the day or into the meeting.

Rightly Parsers, outfitted with the FACTS, STORIES, AND BELIEFS PRIME, know that it is futile to debate the facts and/or listen to stories when a group is fragmented. They shift the conversation to explore the participants' underlying beliefs and why individuals hold them so tightly. This shift is crucial to getting the group unstuck.

When people discuss beliefs openly, they lose their grip on a group. Revealing beliefs allows group members to engage naturally in a more productive examination in which they actively distinguish facts from stories from beliefs.

The following are five steps to outfit yourself with the FACTS, STORIES, AND BELIEFS PRIME and become a Rightly Parser:

1. Practice and get good at discerning FACTS from STORIES from BELIEFS. The next time you are in a discussion, actively code what people are saying as one of these.

2. Recognize that it is useless to argue at the fact level. People can always lash together a subset of all available facts to compose a story that validates a belief they already hold.

3. Ask people to share the beliefs behind their point of view. Once people reveal these, help them realize that their beliefs are just that—beliefs. Yes, they are *their* current truths. But they may not be *the* truth.

4. Then, get the group to state three to seven beliefs they all share. Shared beliefs are not that hard to define. People all over the world generally have the same set of values, so start looking there (see CULTURE PRIME).

5. Once you have stated a few shared beliefs, help the group examine the facts and tell stories from the lens of these shared beliefs. This will help the group form meaningful and sustainable agreements.

The FACTS, STORIES, AND BELIEFS PRIME does require discipline. Distinguishing facts from stories from beliefs takes effort. But now that you understand the distinction that this PRIME reveals, you will naturally apply it and switch into rightly parsing when the stakes are high and you care deeply about the discussion's outcome.

Fire and swords are slow engines of destruction,
compared to the tongue of a Gossip.

           Sir Richard Steele[2]

GOSSIP

GOSSIP

What is it? What makes it so destructive? How do you stop it?

In this context, GOSSIP is defined as when two (or more) people talk about a third person . . . in a manner that leaves the third person diminished in his or her eyes with no one doing the talking committed to helping the third person directly.

GOSSIP is pure, negative energy that destroys possibility and is the most harmful behavior any group can choose to tolerate.

However, GOSSIP is tolerated in most organizations. Attempts to eliminate it often prove ineffective because the efforts are focused on eliminating the "saying" of GOSSIP. The problem with this approach is that many people fail in the moment to recognize that they are spreading GOSSIP.

If you want to build a GOSSIP-free culture, you must instead focus on eliminating the "listening" to GOSSIP—because GOSSIP stops when no one listens. It's as simple as this: When anyone begins to complain or talk badly about another person, no matter the reason, ask, "Before you go on, will either of us approach him directly about this?" If the answer is "no," stop listening. Elimination of GOSSIP creates the possibility of sustaining a CULTURE in which group members actively invest in the development of all other members.

When you're up to something big, a CULTURE of zero-tolerance for GOSSIP is critical.

And it ought to be remembered that there is nothing more difficult to take in hand, more perilous to conduct, or more uncertain in its success, than to take the lead in the introduction of a new order of things. Because the innovator has for enemies all those who have done well under the old conditions, and lukewarm defenders in those who may do well under the new. This coolness arises partly from fear of the opponents, who have the laws on their side, and partly from the incredulity of men, who do not readily believe in new things until they have had a long experience of them.

᭜ Niccolo Machiavelli[3]

PART 4

UNIVERSAL PATTERNS OF GROUP FAILURE

How good are you at anticipating, avoiding, and slaying the dragons that inevitably show up and threaten your group and the outcomes your group is standing for?

In the first three parts of *The PRIMES*, we focused on leading in uncertain times, forming powerful alliances, and achieving outstanding group performance. The 30 PRIMES revealed so far outfit you for proactively preparing yourself—and the groups of which you are a part—for success. Part 4 will arm you to deal with the inevitable resistance and dilemmas you will face. It will also help you recognize and circumvent a tendency to just "hide out" when the going gets tough.

It bears reminding that the status quo is ruthless and does not like to be threatened. As stated earlier in this book, more than 8 out of 10 technical projects, problem-solving attempts, and organizational transformation efforts that affect and involve a significant number of stakeholders fail outright. Half of those that cross the finish line fail to meet minimum expectations at the outset and almost exceed budget and schedule.

The good news is that groups tend to harm themselves in rather predictable patterns. The 12 PRIMES revealed in Part 4 serve to forewarn you of these patterns and allow you to predict and avoid these problems—or at the very least nip them in the bud.

New and stirring ideas are belittled, because if they are not belittled the humiliating question arises, "Why, then, are you not taking part in them?"

❦ H. G. Wells[1]

CHAPTER 11

OVERCOMING RESISTANCE

Are you okay with favoring some people and ignoring others?

While most people resist change, the patterns of this resistance are fairly predictable. By understanding these patterns, you can channel a significant portion of the energy spent resisting the change into energy that instead drives it. And you can learn alternately to recognize and ignore sources of insignificant resistance.

High-performing groups have learned to distinguish which people resisting the change matter and which ones do not. They spend the maximum amount of time working with the first group and virtually ignore the latter group. This skill is teachable.

Michael Doyle had a unique way of seeing resistance to change; he considered it evidence that the change effort was beginning to threaten the status quo. He worried that absence of resistance meant that we weren't doing anything significant. We once received a call from a client who wanted to discuss some strongly worded messages she had received from some of her middle managers regarding the transformation effort. Michael responded by shouting, "Finally, people are beginning to take what we are doing seriously!"

In that spirit, you must embrace resistance while not allowing it to defeat you. The following three PRIMES will show you how.

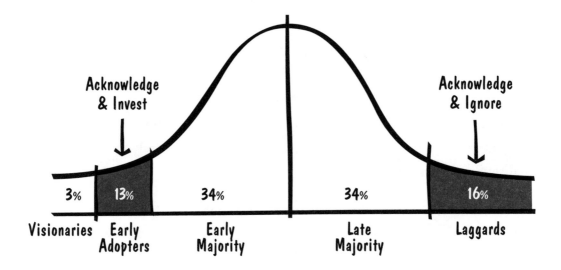

LAGGARDS

LAGGARDS

Do you know how to starve "possibility killers"?

The curve in the LAGGARDS illustration categorizes and quantifies how people react to change. Three percent of your people are "visionaries" who will jump at anything. However, they have limited credibility among other group members. Early Adopters are willing to take a risk if basic questions are answered satisfactorily. The Early Majority relies on Early Adopters for direction, while the Late Majority moves because it doesn't want to be left behind. LAGGARDS, however, never come along; they destroy possibility by constantly asking questions, ignoring answers, and declaring why things won't work.

Leaders must identify the traits of individuals in a group; they have to ignore the LAGGARDS and invest their time and energy in the Early Adopters.

Visionaries stand out right away. These people are the first to sign up when a group is considering a change or introducing a new system. In essence, they are risk junkies—the first to embrace new thoughts, technology, and processes. But their hit rate is low, and their instant enthusiasm can give leadership a false sense of support. Visionaries are easily distracted by the next bright and shiny object. Even though everyone loves to invite visionaries to parties, they would never ask one to cover their backs. They handle risk recklessly and everyone knows it.

When presented with a new idea or change, Early Adopters ask important questions: "What does this new possibility mean? How is it going to affect our existing market share? What are we going to do with our existing products?" They ask good questions, need good answers, and listen; they want to be convinced. When Early Adopters' questions are answered satisfactorily, they say, "Okay, we don't have it all worked out yet, but we have enough information to move. I am in."

As soon as Early Adopters move, the Early Majority moves in right behind them. They have their hearts in the right place and want to do what's right for the organization, but they rely on the Early Adopters to do all their thinking.

The Late Majority's only desire is to avoid being left behind. As soon as the Early Majority moves, members of this group follow. They do not really know what is going on or what all this change stuff means, but they want to be part of the movement, whatever it is.

Initially, LAGGARDS are difficult to distinguish from Early Adopters. They too ask good questions when presented with a change or new way of doing things. They are often well prepared and smart. Their major distinction is that they remain in place and ask more questions, even after the Early Adopters and their followers move out. LAGGARDS rarely enroll fully in a universe-denting effort. They drag their feet and often need to be carried. They love getting attention; it fuels their resistance.

It used to be that transformational leaders were responsible for converting LAGGARDS into the Late or Early Majorities. But that belief was a trap. LAGGARDS appoint themselves as guardians of the status quo; they aim to protect it from an uncertain future. They don't realize or accept that they can *create* the future.

LAGGARDS draw attention to themselves by taking the air out of any possibility under the pretense of "I just want to make sure we do the right thing." They show up at the worst time with "secret knowledge."

After years of trying to bring LAGGARDS on board, we've learned simply to ignore them. Whenever they start to talk, look right into their eyes and move closer and closer to them until you are almost touching noses. Furl your eyebrows for additional effect. The second they stop talking, say, "Got it! Jerry, what do you think?" Who is Jerry? If he is an Early Adopter, you are right to ask him what he thinks. You want to involve Early Adopters in such conversations.

Your ability to reach your goal depends on your ability to distinguish LAGGARDS from Early Adopters as quickly as possible and to pour your energy into the latter group. When the Early Adopters move, everyone you need moves behind them. If you have 10 hours in a day, invest 11 in Early Adopters. They're your best constituency.

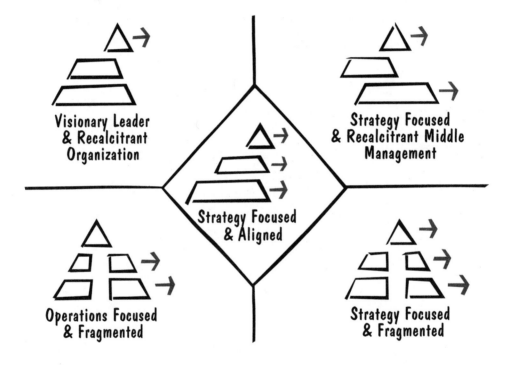

FRAGMENTATION

FRAGMENTATION

*How skilled are you at overcoming resistance
from the powerful middle?*

FRAGMENTATION is the splitting of focus and commitment among stakeholders. A noticeable crack in the group's intentionality appears. A few in the group even begin to question why the expedition was undertaken in the first place. There's no longer unity of purpose, solidarity, or commitment to the vision.

FRAGMENTATION usually happens at the worst possible time. It's essential to recognize the beginnings of FRAGMENTATION. In order to reestablish cohesion, leaders must act quickly and effectively.

When faced with new possibilities, people react in predictable ways. The FRAGMENTATION PRIME helps a leader to visualize what kind of splintering is occurring.

Let's examine the patterns in the illustration of the FRAGMENTATION PRIME:

- The center represents the ideal condition: The leaders move out, and the middle and lower levels of the group follow nicely.

• The top left of the illustration shows leaders who moved ahead without enrolling anyone in the group. This is a lonely place for leadership and typically does not end well. When a group finds itself alone, the vision may be lost, and the entire project could fail. The leader must rally the team.

• The bottom left section illustrates a mutiny. The leader and some of the team members at lower levels are entrenched in the status quo. They failed to internalize the STAKE, and they aren't motivated to change anything. Others take matters into their own hands and move out on their own.

• The upper right corner of the illustration shows a leader who has inspired the rank and file but who hasn't communicated the benefits effectively to middle managers. This type of FRAGMENTATION is prevalent in government, where leaders come and go every 18 months while career managers remain in place. If managers don't like what they hear, they adopt a "this-too-shall-pass" attitude. Underestimation of the power of the middle team is a rookie leader's most costly error.

• The most common type of FRAGMENTATION is seen at the bottom right of the illustration. In this case, the leader has rallied the team at all levels, yet some have chosen to protect the status quo. As the top moves out, the middle and bottom levels of the group split. Some move with the leader toward the vision, while others resist. This tenuous circumstance must be handled with extreme care.

There are many solutions to the problems that FRAGMENTATION creates. As soon as you realize which group or groups you need to align, use the most applicable PRIMES to reestablish COHESION and move forward as a unit. The most important insight to be gained from this

PRIME is that the middle has tremendous power to either drive or destroy a change effort—more power than the leader. There is almost always some FRAGMENTATION in the middle. The key is to determine whether the resisters are LAGGARDS or Early Adopters. If they are Early Adopters, you must address this situation immediately; if they are LAGGARDS, you can simply ignore them (as discussed in the previous section).

SAME—DIFFERENT

SAME–DIFFERENT

Everybody's special. Really?

One of the largest sources of resistance to large-scale collaboration is each person's *belief* that he or she is special and has unique needs that other members of the group do not share. The idea of using a common system or process scares these people; they don't think such an approach will accommodate their individual needs. The SAME–DIFFERENT PRIME can help people get over this fear.

Each of the three images in the SAME–DIFFERENT PRIME represent the structure of an enterprise. The box at the bottom shows the part that is consistent across operating units, while the stacks represent the parts that are unique to each one. For example, the one on the left with the tall stacks would represent a firm like GE, while a brand like McDonald's is represented on the right. GE gives its operating units, like the jet engine division, GE Finance, and GE Home Appliances, a terrific amount of operating discretion (the tall stacks). But GE has a consistent way of running its finances (the small shared box at the bottom). McDonald's, on the other hand, gives almost no discretion to its operating units (the short stacks). Each restaurant looks and behaves almost exactly like any other McDonald's restaurant (the large shared box). Neither approach is right or wrong; both of these companies are very successful. They are simply structured differently.

The general design of the SAME–DIFFERENT PRIME helps you realize how agreements among different stakeholders are facilitated. Start by showing stakeholders the SAME–DIFFERENT

PRIME and ask them what they think it means. Most groups figure this out. Then ask them which of the three models best represents their current situation. They will typically choose the one on the extreme left or, less frequently, the middle model. Then ask them to list all the things they share, and write these in the box. Ask them what is unique, and record these on their corresponding stack.

Next, challenge each item they have listed as unique. Investigate whether these attributes stem from tradition or are, in fact, essential. See if they can find ways to move their stated "differences" into the "same" box. The more they can do this, the larger the space for collaboration and economy-of-scale solutions becomes.

Keep in mind that each retailer used to have its own credit system. Now retailers all use the same credit card authorization system. Travel agents used to use their custom reservation systems. Now more than 55,000 travel agency locations, 400 airlines, 88,000 hotels, 24 car rental brands, and 13 cruise lines operate using a shared system called SABRE. Grocers each had their own pricing systems. Now they all use the Universal Price Code (UPC) solution. We sometimes forget that in order for these and similar solutions to be possible now, hundreds of fragmented stakeholders had to surrender their uniqueness and embrace a "same" way of doing business.

The SAME–DIFFERENT PRIME actually became part of US federal law. The George W. Bush administration hired my company to help put US government services online. Our country was falling behind the rest of the world in delivering government services via the Internet—and we were losing ground. Our initial analysis quickly showed that individual government agencies were putting their services into web portals. We then used the LEVELS OF PERSPECTIVE PRIME to look at the totality of the efforts. We could see from this "system-level" view that, for example, 22 federal agencies were building web portals to administer grant programs—and each was doing so in its special way. In other words, a citizen would have to interface with 22 unique systems.

Users would do best having a single interface, which we called www.GRANTS.GOV. Because many of the agencies conveyed strong resistance to standardization, we used the SAME–DIFFERENT PRIME to explain the circumstances throughout the Office of Management and Budget and the Congress. Eventually, the E-GOV law passed, making it mandatory for government agencies to work together (thus moving the federal government more to the right side of the SAME–DIFFERENT PRIME).

Use this PRIME to help support members of the group when they are trying to determine whether they think standardization is appropriate. Keep the conversation away from right and wrong, and think of it instead as managing tension.

Chapter 12 will present three PRIMES that reveal how to manage these right versus right dilemmas.

Life is a constant oscillation between the sharp thorns of dilemmas.

                                              H. L. Mencken[1]

CHAPTER 12

MANAGING INTRACTABLE DILEMMAS

How do you end a never-ending argument?

You are about to meet the first, most often applied, and easiest to understand PRIME—and one that was so horribly mismanaged during the end of the twentieth century and beginning of the twenty-first century that we experienced a global financial collapse. The PRIME is called BIG HAT–LITTLE HAT. Michael Doyle had already been using it with groups for over 15 years when he introduced it to me in 1986. It was the first PRIME I learned to draw, and it is the one I draw most often today. BIG HAT–LITTLE HAT represents the tension between "good for me" versus "good for all."

You are also going to learn about BIG HAT–LITTLE HAT's three siblings, which together represent the four most common intractable dilemmas that have been tearing groups apart since ancient times. As such, we turned to the ancient scholars to find the resolution principles to these dilemmas.

Mastering the three PRIMES revealed in this chapter will allow you to quickly recognize when people are arguing over a right versus right clash of values and trying to prove each other wrong in the process. You will be able to intervene to show them how futile this approach is. Finally, you will be able to shift their perspective from "I am right and you are wrong" to one where they work together with the resolution principles to find the "most right" solution.

BIG HAT–LITTLE HAT

BIG HAT—LITTLE HAT

*What do you do when the needs of the many conflict
with the needs of the few?*

BIG HAT–LITTLE HAT represents a powerful right versus right dilemma that groups confront constantly. It's fun to put on a BIG HAT, think like the CEO, and make decisions that are good for the company. It's natural and unavoidable, however, to put on a LITTLE HAT and assess how corporate actions impact your unit or local operation. People who wear these two hats will never see the same issue in the same way. And until you name both viewpoints, the conflict between them will be pervasive—yet relatively invisible.

BIG HAT–LITTLE HAT once plagued a transformation initiative at the US Army National Guard (ARNG) taking place at the closing of the twentieth century. At that time Major General William Navas was the Director of the ARNG and a passionate leader with a deep understanding of the US Constitution and the framers' intent. When General Navas directed the Guard, it was made up of 360,000 soldiers under the leadership of 54 adjutant generals (TAGS). Most of the time, the TAGS reported to the state governors. This structure was Thomas Jefferson's way of ensuring that the President couldn't send troops in against the states. In time of war, however, the Guard could be mobilized under federal control.

Since its inception, the National Guard has functioned with this embedded split. On the one hand, it's a collection of 54 armies, free to make independent decisions in their respective state's best interests. On the other hand, it's a military force that must snap to alignment with the US Army. General Navas was responsible for making all this work.

The TAGS wore SMALL HATS when they made choices in the best interests of their particular states. They wore BIG HATS when they joined General Navas in his effort to modernize and transform the entire system within the confines of severely constrained budgets. Our team provided the consultants to support General Navas's initiative—and the STAKES were high. General Navas was most concerned that if he couldn't build cohesive intent and focus within the TAG community, negotiations with the Pentagon regarding the budget would become more difficult than they already were.

Under General Navas's direction, we employed the principle that "What you resist persists." We embraced the BIG HAT–LITTLE HAT dilemma. We hung a huge sketch of the PRIME on the wall in the planning room and then dissected its component parts.

Once we delineated the elements of BIG HAT–LITTLE HAT, we asked the group to self-regulate and give out yellow and red cards for inappropriate LITTLE HAT behavior. New values quickly emerged, and the group began to move away from exclusive, "either/or" solutions and to search for inclusive, "both/and" solutions.

The BIG HAT–LITTLE HAT PRIME reveals:

- The argument is right versus right as opposed to right versus wrong.

- We cannot eliminate the implicit dichotomy of this PRIME; we can only manage it.

- People need to be clear about which hat they are wearing when they speak.

- It is fair to advocate for your LITTLE HAT, but not to the detriment of the whole.

It is essential that people agree not to threaten the BIG HAT'S existence. A unit has no right to hurt the whole system.

The TAGS came together and figured out the National Guard transformation. Their solidarity was evident in the plans and budgets they built and in the negotiations they had with the Department of Defense. These same plans and budgets are now considered an integral part of America's Army, while National Guard troops maintain their vital role as state-based first responders at the service of the governors.

Leaders must become adept at wearing BIG HATS and LITTLE HATS to manage groups effectively through right versus right challenges. BIG HAT–LITTLE HAT remains one of the top-four challenges that appear along the path to transformative outcomes. The next PRIME reveals the other three.

Out beyond right and wrong there is a green field.
I'll meet you there.

꿍 Rumi[1]

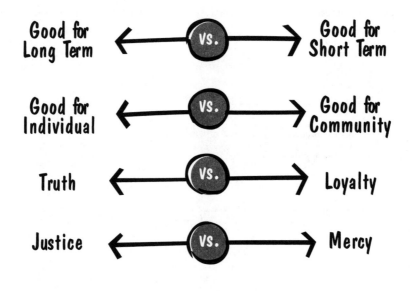

RIGHT VERSUS RIGHT

RIGHT versus RIGHT

Resolving conflicts about right and wrong is child's play.
How skilled are you at resolving matters of right versus right?

When conversations deteriorate into disagreements that disintegrate into arguments, the great misperception is that one position must be right and others must be wrong. While right versus wrong issues certainly create opportunities for disagreement, it can be as debilitating and destructive as gossip to mistake a RIGHT versus RIGHT issue for a right versus wrong dilemma. It is imperative to recognize immediately the collision of two "rights"; this recognition enables a leader to intervene, honor all the "rights," and reorient the group toward the defined "To Be."

The power of right versus right dilemmas, the four most divisive of which are noted in the PRIME illustration, was first revealed to me by Rushworth Kidder of the Institute for Global Ethics in Rockland, Maine.[2] I sought out Dr. Kidder in response to a request by one of our senior clients. The client noticed an increasing incidence of inappropriate, immoral, and, at times, illegal behavior among some personnel. He wanted an external review of his organization's stated values as a way to begin to address the worrisome trends.

Dr. Kidder pointed out that an organization's values are rarely the source of ethical problems. His research showed that, throughout the world, core values are almost universal. For example, "truth" and "loyalty" are highly prized across almost all societies. Serious problems arise, however, when these values—these "rights"—collide. Here's a perfect example of colliding rights: How are personnel instructed to behave, for example, when a superior orders a subordinate to lie? The subordinate faces an intractable dilemma between loyalty to the superior and being truthful.

You will recognize RIGHT VERSUS RIGHT dilemmas everywhere. What happens when the needs of the group are in conflict with the needs of a specific individual? These issues confront us throughout the human experience.

Consider little Susie, whose parents teach her to be a good friend and always tell the truth. What happens when Susie's third-grade teacher asks her if her best friend, Tommy, just copied the answers from her test? Susie knows he did. Does loyalty to Tommy trump loyalty to the truth, or vice versa?

In his book *How Good People Make Tough Choices*, Kidder makes clear the ethical dilemmas we face every day. The first step in managing these challenges is to recognize them when they occur. By naming these RIGHT VERSUS RIGHT dilemmas, we make them visible and recognizable.

No single answer exists to resolve RIGHT VERSUS RIGHT dilemmas. The next PRIME, however—for which Rush Kidder deserves all the credit—shows how to handle and resolve colliding rights. Resolution is critical because getting stuck and standing still for too long can effectively destroy your efforts.

. . . the secret that has puzzled all the philosophers, baffled all the lawyers, muddled all the men of business, and ruined most of the artists: the secret of right and wrong.

            ❧ George Bernard Shaw[3]

RESOLUTION PRINCIPLES

RESOLUTION PRINCIPLES

Right versus right arguments have been going on forever.
What can we learn from our ancestors?

You'll likely encounter one or more dilemmas on the path to your declared outcome. The RESOLUTION PRINCIPLES PRIME can help you find the highest "right" when faced with the toughest choices.

Every leader has faced the challenge of handling an underperforming employee. This dilemma is particularly difficult when extenuating circumstances (for example, factors outside the person's control such as family or health issues) contribute to a lack of performance. Such a situation puts managers squarely between their "compassionate" desire to do what is "right" for the individual and their "just" desire to do what is "right" for the organization—as well as any other employees who bear the burden of the underperformance.

There are only three ways to make the best choice when faced with such a RIGHT versus RIGHT dilemma:

1.   **End-based:** Select the option that generates the most good for the most people.

2.   **Rule-based:** Choose as if you're creating a universal standard.

3.   **Care-based:** Choose as if you were the one most affected by your decision.

As Rumi said: "Out beyond right and wrong, there is a green field. I'll meet you there."

Ethical dilemmas are unavoidable and often hidden from view. To resolve them with others is a distinct and potentially rich human experience. We do such a service to the people with whom we work when we first help them see the situation for what it is and then make explicit the three RESOLUTION PRINCIPLES. Once we clarify these principles, people tend to choose the one most applicable to their situation. There is no wrong answer here. It is simply a choice.

We would rather be ruined than changed; We would rather die in our dread than climb the cross of the moment and let our illusions die.

❧ W. H. Auden[4]

CHAPTER 13

AVOIDING TRIPPING HAZARDS

Tripping hazards are easier to avoid when you know where they are. When it comes to working in groups, can you see them coming?

This chapter will reveal three of the most common tripping hazards that take groups off track. Tripping hazards are like blind spots in that they no longer pose a threat once you know where they are.

After mastering Chapter 13's PRIMES, you will not waste your time on academic leadership development and team-building investments. You will know that the skills of leadership and teamwork are forged in the real work—where there is real cost to failure.

You will also be able to distinguish process from content among collaborating groups and ensure that whoever is responsible for the process must surrender his or her right to contribute content.

Finally, you will never be tempted to make a decision during a planning or problem-solving meeting.

This discipline will require little effort because you will understand the futility of going down any other path and the harmful effects of forgetting what these PRIMES reveal.

Coming together is a beginning. Keeping together is progress. Working together is success.

          ✤ Henry Ford[1]

CHASE–LOSE

CHASE–LOSE

*Chase teamwork, leadership, morale, and culture and you will surely lose
them all.*

I've always been fascinated with high-performance teams, cultures, and leaders. In the last 20 years, I've done a fair amount of team building and leadership coaching. CHASE–LOSE revealed itself slowly to me over time. This PRIME has profoundly affected how I approach problem solving, transformation, team building, culture creation, and leadership development today because it reveals a seemingly counterintuitive truth: Often what we CHASE is not what we catch. It has become popular in recent years to seek certain admirable qualities in business operations. CHASE–LOSE reveals the fallacy that their pursuit will lead to success.

When we CHASE team, we LOSE team.

When we CHASE culture, we LOSE culture.

When we CHASE leadership, we LOSE leadership.

When we CHASE innovation, we LOSE innovation.

This PRIME illuminates the fact that teamwork, innovation, leadership, and all the other characteristics of high-performance CULTURE are not ends in themselves. Rather, they are skills and competencies that we refine during the relentless pursuit of extraordinary outcomes. CHASE–LOSE puts work and the nature of work in the right order.

Instead of CHASING the characteristics of high-performance CULTURE, this principle guides leaders and groups to:

- CHASE a meaningful outcome.

- Deal quickly with whatever puts that outcome at risk by quickly intervening to teach a best practice or stop a destructive practice.

- Achieve the outcomes and improve our CULTURE at the same time.

Here's an example of how these three guidelines were applied to a transformational initiative that produced extraordinary results and put a significant dent in the universe:

In spring 2001, President George W. Bush declared E-Gov—the use of the Internet to transform the way government operates and delivers services (see the SAME–DIFFERENT PRIME)—one of his top administrative priorities. The United States had slipped behind dozens of countries in its E-Gov ranking. Under the direction of Mark Forman, the federal government's Chief Information Officer at the time, our team was assigned to develop sweeping new E-Gov applications. The track record of projects like this was atrocious and we faced two diametrically opposed facts right away:

1. The biggest gains to be made required cross-government collaboration.

2. Nothing in the structure of the federal government promoted such collaboration.

At the behest of the Executive Office, we asked each agency to give us one of its best and brightest people to participate in Project Quicksilver. We gave the 75 or so who were selected a big room, computers, flip charts, coffee and juice, and a hundred days to figure out the fewest, most important projects that, with sufficient resources and leadership, the United States could complete in a year.

Initially, Quicksilver members were guarded and skeptical. They had seen initiatives like this come and go for years. Soon, only 73 days were left, then 51, then 39. They knew their recommendations would go directly to the President's Management Council and the senior leadership of the Office of Management and Budget on the 100th day.

The group's effectiveness increased as the available time decreased and the clock ticked on; they dealt with issues that put the outcome at risk—leadership, teamwork, culture—more quickly. They distinguished LAGGARDS from Early Adopters, ignored the former, and had the latter take on added responsibility as the group approached its midpoint. FRAGMENTATION within the group surfaced routinely, was quickly addressed, and recurred just as quickly. The clock kept ticking, and the stakes stayed high.

Then, it happened: About 70 days into the 100-day project, I entered the Quicksilver area at midmorning. The place smelled of coffee...and possibility. Someone had brought fresh bagels and cream cheese, I noticed, as my eyes opened wider to the amazing display of high-performance collaboration that surrounded me. Some people were huddled in small, intense groups. Others were gathered around a computer, engrossed in their effort to make sense of the numbers displayed on the screen. People even sat together on the floor, where they mapped something out on a long sheet of paper. No longer were these stray individuals from different government agencies: They were Quicksilver, a high-performance team at work to solve real problems that faced our country. They met the deadline and delivered hundreds of projects to be considered, 22 of which were ultimately selected, funded, and implemented over the following year. The United States went from ranking somewhere in the 30s to number one in the world in the use of the Internet to operate and deliver government services.

As program managers for the Quicksilver project, we never CHASED any direct team-building, leadership development, or innovation practices. We didn't host any workshops to facilitate CULTURE creation. We simply dealt immediately with anything that put the outcome at risk.

CHASE–LOSE sets the right order to things:

- First, answer the call and respond to big challenges.

- Next, enroll others and declare your intentions with integrity.

- Then, get busy and work as quickly as possible.

- Finally, deal quickly with anything that threatens success.

The right order ensures that you have an opportunity to be part of a high-performance team, experience the profound privilege of leading powerfully, and make your dent in the universe.

If we are always arriving and departing, it is also true that we are eternally anchored. One's destination is never a place but rather a new way of looking at things.

                                  ❧ Henry Miller[2]

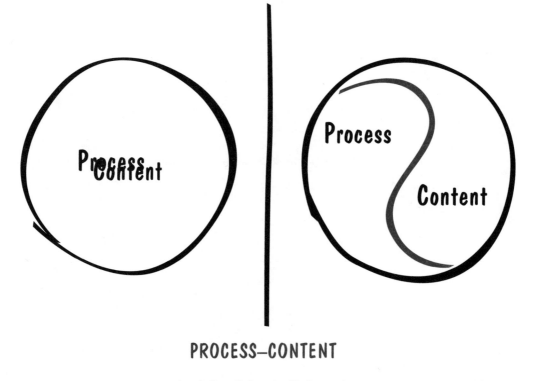

PROCESS–CONTENT

PROCESS–CONTENT

You can run the process. You can contribute to content. Pick one.

If you work with a group that has more than seven participants, someone has to facilitate the process. And whoever takes responsibility for facilitating the process *must* surrender his or her right to offer content. Unfortunately, people constantly violate this PRIME.

I regularly see senior leaders running meetings. They facilitate the process while offering content *and* assigning value to what is being said. This is completely inappropriate; it does not prompt the best ideas to come forward with the best buy-in from stakeholders.

The reason for this is simple: If you are running the process and have a stake in the outcome, you will manipulate the process to get your outcome. When the stakes are high and many stakeholders are involved, process and content must be separated. Someone must be held responsible for designing a well-thought-out process design and make that design explicit and fair.

That same person then must facilitate the process so that participants are treated fairly. Whoever is taking this very important role must surrender his or her right to add content. I call this period of time "in role neutral." This person agrees to go into a role of service to the group, give up advocating for a specific set of ideas, and support adherence to the process.

This person must be explicit when he or she is temporarily stepping into and out of this job. This is a role that a person is willing to take on for a limited period of time; it is not who the person is.

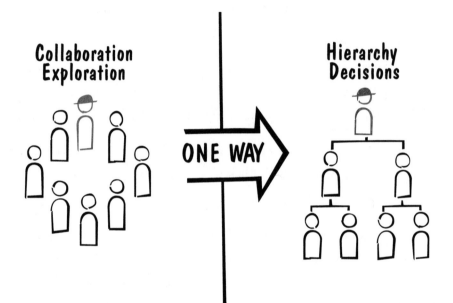

SHAPE SHIFTING

SHAPE SHIFTING

How to destroy your power in groups.

Meetings are rarely the best place to make decisions. They are, however, a good place to develop recommendations that can later turn into decisions. Leaders can assume a collaborative or an authoritarian relationship with a group, but not both at once. How explicit are you about your role?

Every group needs and wants a leader. Two of the many types of leaders are characterized in this PRIME:

1. Leaders who put themselves into a collaborative relationship with their group: They roll up their sleeves, brainstorm as peers, and help formulate recommendations before the decision is made.

2. Leaders who assume a hierarchical relationship with the group and use their organizational authority to make decisions: They frequently use the command-and-control leadership style mentioned in the LEADERSHIP SPECTRUM PRIME.

Both roles are vital; the key is for leaders to make it clear which role they take. Many make the common mistake of declaring a collaborative relationship with the group and then making authoritative decisions. This change in roles is called SHAPE SHIFTING and it frequently erodes the trust a group places in its leader.

Some decisions necessitate creativity, innovation, and the group's involvement and wisdom, while other situations require a quick decision.

The discussion of OPEN–CLOSE–DECIDE showed us that there's no such thing as "group" decision making. Effective leaders understand how decisions are made and use both types of leadership described here. You must be as skilled in collaboration as you are in command-and-control relationships with your team. The SHAPE SHIFTING PRIME reveals potential dangers as you navigate between these two styles.

Here's an example of a SHAPE SHIFT: A leader declares a collaborative relationship to generate ideas. Then, caught up in the spirit of the exchange, he or she suddenly shouts, "That's a terrible idea. Forget that one." Or just as destructively, "Bill, that's a great idea! We've got the budget. Let's do it!" Instantly, no matter how the chairs are arranged, a hierarchy overtakes the process. The leader SHAPE SHIFTED and used his or her organizational authority to behave differently from everyone else. He valued an idea, resourced it in his or her mind, and passed judgment in public.

The room is now a boardroom, and everyone knows it. People who have unexpressed ideas shut down immediately. They no longer trust the process. The group becomes guarded and won't go back to collaboration. Group members worry that their ideas will be judged in public and refuse to open themselves up to possible embarrassment.

To avoid the often-fatal mistake of SHAPE SHIFTING, you must adhere to four best practices:

1.   Distinguish between collaboration with the group and a command-and-control relationship. Master the best practices of each.

2.   Intentionally and explicitly choose one role or the other in any given situation.

3.   Don't shift from one role to another. Forewarn the group explicitly if you must shift—typically from collaboration to command and control. Remember, it's almost impossible to return to collaboration once the shift to command and control has been made.

4.   Don't shift relationships with group members during the course of any single meeting. Collaborate with them one day but resist the temptation to make any decisions or pass unilateral judgment on a particular idea. Collaboration typically generates recommendations as opposed to decisions. After careful consideration of the recommendations, use your organizational authority on a later day to make a decision.

What you resist persists.

        ❧ Michael Doyle

REFUSING TO HIDE OUT

We all live our lives trying to avoid embarrassment. Can you recognize when you and your group are hiding out and playing safe?

Take a minute to remember the first time you ever felt embarrassed or shamed in front of others. Most people have no trouble bringing the disturbing memory back up to consciousness. What most people do not know is that from that moment on, you spent your life trying to make sure you never put yourself in a position where you might have that feeling again.

Somewhere along the way, as you and your group pursue your "declared date-certain outcome," you will probably become discouraged. Things are not going as planned and just seem too hard. But you cannot admit it's your fault you might fail for fear of shame and embarrassment. For those who choose, there are three convenient places to hide out so that you can fail to produce your declared outcome but not get blamed. Most people do not know they are hiding out; however, you realize this if you master the following three PRIMES. You will also know that everybody who reads this book *knows* you are hiding out. (Sometimes ignorance really is bliss.)

The next three PRIMES will reveal the following: First, you will sense when you and the group are giving up your power to others and "going victim"—and you will know how to stop this from happening. Second, you will know that there is no risk in planning and growing anxious when excessive time is spent *talking* about taking action rather than actually taking action. Finally, you will understand the limited value of performance metrics that report "how well the team did." You will crave metrics that "project" how the team thinks it is going to do and intervene as appropriate. In short, the next three PRIMES make it hard to hide out.

Change has a considerable psychological impact on the human mind. To the fearful it is threatening because it means things may get worse. To the hopeful it is encouraging because things may get better. To the confident it is inspiring because the challenge exists to make things better.

                   ❧ King Whitney, Jr[1]

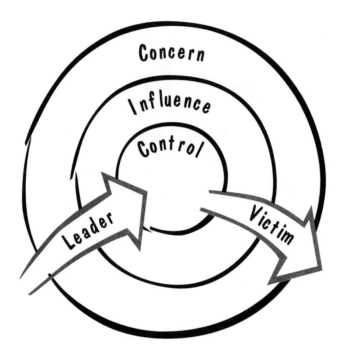

VICTIM—LEADER

VICTIM–LEADER

What does "going victim" sound like?

Great leaders and high-performance teams listen carefully to the tone and direction of their conversations. They can identify when a group begins to lose its power by complaining about things it cannot affect and blaming others for its own lack of effectiveness. This is the sound of a victim: "If Congress would just do its job, we could do ours." You cannot gain anything by wishing that things we can't control were different.

Good leaders identify when groups operate from a sense of empowerment and a can-do attitude; great leaders help victim-oriented groups regain their power and help empowered groups sustain theirs. The VICTIM–LEADER PRIME is the "nuclear PRIME" because groups hate it when it is brought to their attention, and they resent the person who revealed it. This is because it is, of course, much easier to be a VICTIM than to be a LEADER.

Groups are moving toward being LEADERS or VICTIMS at any single point in time. They talk either about things they can do or about what's being done to them. Once it can distinguish this PRIME, a group becomes directly responsible for tolerating victimhood. This awareness makes what once was easy—hiding out and blaming others—suddenly unpleasant and intolerable.

To take responsibility at all times—to be the cause—may feel like a huge burden. VICTIM–LEADER therefore is one of the few PRIMES best introduced in explicit fashion sparingly. This PRIME is valuable even when you keep it to yourself. So even if you don't speak of it, pay close attention to which way the group is headed. Guide group members to talk about things they can control. That's where their power is stored.

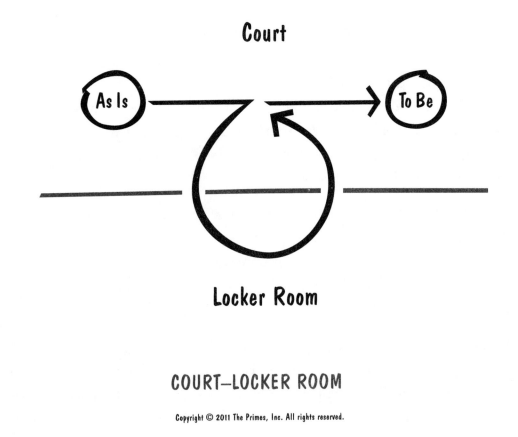

COURT—LOCKER ROOM

COURT—LOCKER ROOM

Do you find planning to be a near-death experience?

Planning is a near-death experience. We step out of living (COURT), and we step into talking about living (LOCKER ROOM). At best, planning helps us become organized and take action. In the business environment, it more often serves as giving us something to do so we do not have to actually do anything.

These are strong words to say for someone who makes his living by helping to solve complex problems and drive system-wide change and transformation. Planning is obviously an essential component of this line of work. The problem is that there is no risk in planning. Planning is comfortable. By contrast, when we are on the COURT—committing resources, changing polices, forging new agreements, integrating new systems, releasing new products and services to the market, putting saw to wood, ordering troops to attack—there is huge risk of looking bad, being wrong, being uncomfortable, getting fired, or even getting killed.

This PRIME began to reveal itself when we were asked to support an 18-month transformation effort in Washington, DC. Regular meetings were scheduled for leadership to participate. Near the end of our first planning meeting, with only 30 minutes to go, we asked, "Is there anything obvious that we could take on now to get this transformation started?" People were flustered. They said, "We are only on the first day of this planning process. It is too early to take an action." We asked them, "How long have each of you lived and worked in DC?" Collectively, the number was over 500 years. And so we replied, "We have 500 years of experience and dozens of recent studies. When you close your eyes and imagine DC, isn't there anything obvious, no matter how much longer we study it, that we simply must do now? Because it either *must* be part of our vision for the city or *must not* be part of the city we imagine."

After just a few moments, the city administrator made a suggestion to close DC General, the only public hospital in town. As he explained, "The building is old and loaded with asbestos. We have studied this for years. We know the costs to bring it up to code are simply not worth it."

We encouraged the leadership team to think of the transformation of DC like a basketball game. We will develop an overall game plan. Then we will get onto the court and act. While on the court, depending on what is showing up, we will call some plays and adjust our plan. Sometimes we will stop playing and huddle up for some deeper planning, then get back onto the court. We encouraged these leaders to abandon the idea that we first must make a plan and then execute it. Rather, we have an overall bias to be on the court driving transformation, and only when we feel the need and for no longer than absolutely necessary. We leave the court, go to the locker room, do some planning, and then get back onto the court.

The team bought the idea. One week later, the leadership declared that now was the time to close DC General. And that is what happened. For the next 18 months, we would come together regularly and further develop our DYNAMICALLY INCOMPLETE vision of the city, while at the same time identifying opportunities to get onto the court and take real steps toward our emerging vision.

The LOCKER ROOM–COURT PRIME distinguishes "thinking" from "doing." While both are important, doing is more important and more difficult. Notice the loop from COURT to LOCKER ROOM. This PRIME is revealing in that the real world sometimes surprises people as they work together on the COURT toward a "To Be" state. Occasionally something happens that was not considered in the plan. At this point, the group drops off the COURT to process this new development in the LOCKER ROOM. It's crucial to notice that when you leave the LOCKER ROOM and go back onto the COURT, you start from exactly where you left off.

Look carefully at this PRIME. The group has made a DECLARATION to achieve the date-certain outcome with INTEGRITY. When the unexpected happens and group members drop off the COURT and go to the LOCKER ROOM, the clock keeps ticking; it never stops

DECLARATIVE LEADERSHIP, which creates a sense of urgency. Conversations are fierce. PERIMETERS are expanded, FEEDBACK is flowing, and the group is chomping at the bit to get out of the LOCKER ROOM and back onto the COURT. Oh, what a feeling!

The LOCKER ROOM–COURT PRIME also reveals something about innovation—a big buzzword these days. An emerging industry is one that promises to help companies enhance their capacity to innovate. I witness regularly that people get extremely innovative when they do the following:

- They have clarity about where they are (AS IS), where they are going (TO BE), and why making this move is so important (STAKE) (see CORE PRIME).

- They have declared a specific date-certain outcome with INTEGRITY (see DECLARATION PRIME).

- They are dealing with the unexpected and are running out of time.

This situation ALWAYS causes innovation. I never cease to be amazed by what people imagine and how clever and creative they really can be. The key is to never change the date. The group gave its word. Time is running out. Pressure is building. It is this pressure that drives innovation.

You can put the LOCKER ROOM–COURT PRIME to use with members of your group by first introducing it to them and letting them understand what it reveals. Then, as they move through various activities, help them see when they are on the COURT and when they are in the LOCKER ROOM. Let the PRIME do the work. The group will start to self-adjust. There is no need to force the issue. One thing you will see very quickly is intolerance for status meetings and non-value-added activity (see MUDA).

It is not the mountain we conquer, but ourselves.

~ Sir Edmund Hillary[2]

A Powerful State of Learning

CONFUSION

CONFUSION

Why is confusion such a wonderful way of being?

"How does it feel to be wrong?" This was the question Jennifer Thompson-Cannino, coauthor of *Picking Cotton*, asked a group of us gathered in Camden, Maine. People responded with answers like "embarrassing, humiliating, and humbling." Jennifer then asked us if we were sure that these were some of the feelings we had when we were wrong. We answered, "yes." "Well, you are all wrong," she responded. For the next minute or so, she held the room in silence. We sat there in a state of confusion. We also had a feeling we were about to learn something.

Before we solve this riddle, I want you to deeply reflect on a time when you were wrong. This isn't difficult for most people. Take a piece of paper and write a word or two that describes how being wrong felt to you. If your answers are like ours were, you too are wrong. Confused? Good. Thompson-Cannino went on to explain that "being wrong feels *exactly* like being right...until you *realize* you are wrong."

In the sixth century BC, people believed the earth was flat. They lived their entire lives feeling right but being wrong. Imagine that afternoon when Pythagoras called everybody down to the Great Theatre on the slope of Panayir Hill in Ephesus to reveal a startling revelation: "Hi, everybody. Hey, ya'll know that belief we all have about the earth being flat?" People look from side to side, nodding. "Of course we do!" Then Pythagoras says, "Well, we were wrong on that one." People are shocked and confused. "Yeah, I have proof that the earth is actually round. It's kind of a big mistake we were living there. There is no edge. If we walk east, we will eventually get back to where we stared." This was the moment that people *realized* they were wrong about the flat earth. Before this moment, they were wrong but felt right; after it, they felt and feel right. The only people who got to "feel" wrong were those who went into a conversation believing one thing and came out of the conversation believing something different.

The same phenomenon occurs with every group you lead or are part of. And the same is true about you. Right now, we are all holding on to beliefs that feel right—but are wrong. Before we, as agents of change, can produce shared perspective, shared intent, and synchronized action (POWER PRIME), we must produce impactful moments of confusion. Confusion is a space one must travel through in order to let go of a flawed belief and an overall unknowing, into a right belief and knowing.

The CONFUSION PRIME reveals that confusion is the highest state of learning. In this context, being confused is a state to be appreciated and enjoyed.

There you go man, keep as cool as you can.

Face piles of trials with smiles.

It riles them to believe that you perceive

the web they weave

And keep on thinking free.

                       ∾ The Moody Blues, "In The Beginning,"
from the album On the Threshold of a Dream[3]

PART 5

UNIVERSAL PATTERNS OF THRIVING IN AMBIGUITY

How do you stay healthy when the world is sick?

We end where we began. The future isn't what it used to be. Steady state now is changing at the speed of the environment. To those of you who are frightened to the point of being immobilized, don't worry. I know there are enough of you who see this global reset as the ultimate thrill ride—for which you want a front row seat. You are managers in corporations leading the retooling of our businesses for the new realities. You are engineers designing new ways to harness energy and bring new products to market. You are part of the non-profit world, intent on helping the disenfranchised. You are leading our governments in shaping the new world order. You are students preparing to make your dent in the universe.

Outfitted with the PRIMES, you are ready to step up and answer the call this world is making for people to live huge. You are willing to live unreasonably in leading a rage against the machine. You are a declared enemy of the status quo. Your success hinges on staying healthy and thriving in ambiguity. These final four PRIMES will act as body armor for you and all Universe Denters.

CHAPTER 15

AVOIDING BRIGHT AND SHINY OBJECTS AND SQUIRRELS

How do you manage distractions?

T. S. Eliot once observed that he found himself "distracted from distraction by distraction." In a 2010 *Science* magazine article, Patricia Greenfield, a developmental psychologist who runs UCLA's Children's Digital Media Center, concluded that our growing use of screen-based media is causing "new weaknesses in higher order cognitive processes," including weaknesses in "abstract vocabulary, mindfulness, reflection, inductive problem solving, critical thinking, and imagination." In short, we as people are chronically interrupted. And this problem is going to get much worse as our appliances, vehicles, and even food products vie for our attention.

At the same time, high-performance groups adhere to the advice of Mozart when he said, "The shorter way to do many things is to do only one thing at a time." Bruce Lee speaks truth to those who are taking on the status quo when he advises, "The successful warrior is the average man, with laser-like focus."

The PRIMES in this chapter will outfit you to carve out a space in this over-stimulating environment to give you and your team a mental and physical place to think critically, pursue insights relentlessly, imagine and design innovations, and concentrate deeply on complex problem solving and system transformation.

Know how to listen, and you will profit even from those who talk badly.

         ❧ Plutarch[1]

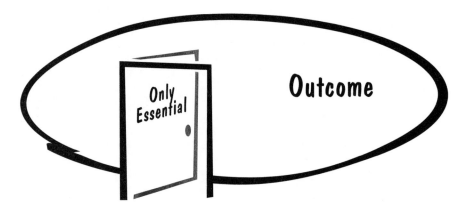

A CLEARING

A CLEARING

How skilled are you at creating nothing?

A CLEARING is a void where nothing exists. You can create CLEARINGS in your schedule or physical CLEARINGS in your office or home or hotel conference center. And you can create CLEARINGS in your mind, as they are spaces where possibilities can exist. In the context of the PRIMES, we remove all facts, thoughts, technology, people, meetings, distractions, interruptions, biases, and legacies. In short, you push aside everything. In this space of nothing, you place your DECLARED OUTCOME. You guard the CLEARING. You let into the CLEARING only what is essential to achieving your DECLARED OUTCOME.

A CLEARING is a place where the fewest people using the least resources can solve problems, drive change, and cause transformation in the least amount of time. People can concentrate in a CLEARING. People can have deep conversations and engage in critical thinking. In a CLEARING, people can do what they are doing.

We are called to solve complicated problems that require deep thinking in order to understand and solve them. Yet we are constantly interrupted by messages and requests for our attention. Consider the following two facts:

1. In 2008, American teens sent and received an average of 80 messages per day, twice the average in 2007.[2]

2.   A 2007 study found that a group of Microsoft workers took an average of 15 minutes to return to serious mental tasks, such as report writing or computer coding, after dealing with incoming e-mail. [3]

Dozens of studies have already been published documenting the negative effects of chronic interruptions and constant requests for our attention via smart phones and computers.

The other problem is that the Internet and computers in general make it so easy for LAGGARDS and other obstructionists to overwhelm a change team with data. People get absolutely paralyzed under the weight of relevant data that "we must consider before acting."

So, create CLEARINGS for your group. Push the noise back. Make an opening where nothing exists except what is essential to your outcome. Here are some tips:

•   Keep your group as small as absolutely possible and try to encourage each person to bring something essential and unique to it.

•   Minimize the amount of data you consider.

•   Get off the grid when you need to do critical thinking. Disconnect from text messages and e-mail as much as you can and manage your connectivity.

The CLEARING PRIME is not about making major life changes. It simply requests that we focus on the task at hand while we're performing it. High-performance groups intentionally build temporary CLEARINGS that are uniquely designed to facilitate the exact project they're completing. Once we've finished, we can take down the CLEARING, and people can choose to do whatever they want. As with the roles people assume in PROCESS–CONTENT, CLEARINGS are not permanent; they are temporary realms of intense focus.

Man is so made that when anything fires his soul, impossibilities vanish.

❧ Jean de la Fontaine[4]

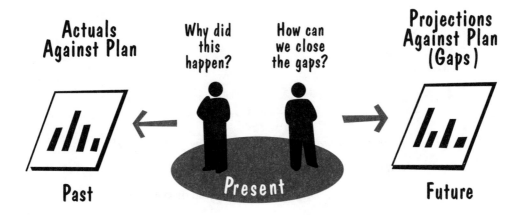

ISSUES FORWARD

ISSUES FORWARD

Looking behind and looking ahead are both important.
What is the right ratio?

Bob Kelly, a senior executive at Arthur Andersen, hosted a gourmet dinner one night in a private dining room of the Jefferson Hotel in Washington, DC. Around the table sat a collection of high-powered, Type-A business leaders who were engaged in a spirited debate about a pressing issue.

A gracious host, Bob listened quietly while the discussion became more intense. As the dessert course arrived amid arguments around the table, Bob raised his hand slowly and said, "ISSUES FORWARD." The room went quiet—and that simple phrase allowed us to redirect our focus to what we could affect and what we needed to do.

Years later, Peter DiGiammarino, then a member of my firm's board of directors, had a similar effect on a conversation and on the way I managed my business. A great teacher and a patient man, Peter helped me understand that leaders look at either performance reports from the past or projections for the future. Most spend their time on performance reports, perhaps because a backward glance is attractive since information is available and confirmed. However, while projections against plan are speculative, they're much more valuable. Two questions leaders must ask about the performance of their organizations or systems are as follows:

Questioning past performance:

1. "What was our plan for last month and how well did we actually meet it?" This question leads to the question "Why did things go that way?" As a form of reflective learning, it's a valuable question.

Questioning future performance:

2.   "What is our plan for next month and what are we currently projecting?" This question leads to the question "What do we have to do now to close the gap between our plan and our projection?"

This question is proactive and leads to actions that influence the future.

Leaders who adopt an ISSUES FORWARD outlook ask in November for December's revenue target and the current projection. Then—and this is the key—they immediately call for action to close the gap between the plan and projection when they spot a potential shortfall. They ask their managers, "What do we have to do now to eliminate the gap between our projection and our plan?" This question illustrates the principle of the ISSUES FORWARD PRIME. Groups can also ensure that they maintain their INTEGRITY by having a shared definition for the following words:

•   Plan: What we intend to make happen at a specific time in the future.

•   Projection: What we think is really going to happen at a specific time unless we do something different.

•   Actuals: What really happened when we look backward and assess.

•   Reforecast: What we do when projections are so far off from plan. We declare a new number to re-establish healthy tension in the system, but we never forget the original plan.

Powerful groups have two ways of assessing their performance. They can compare actual trailing performance with their plan, see the gap, and ask, "Why?" Or they can compare projections with the plan, see the gap, and ask, "How do we close it?" The latter orientation is ISSUES FORWARD and leads to immediate, decisive action.

We cannot wait for the world to turn, for times to change that we might change them, for the revolution to come around and carry us around to its new course. We ourselves are the future.

❧ Beatrice Bruteau[5]

CHAPTER 16

TAKING GREAT CARE
OF YOURSELF

Can you give up coming from "something is wrong"?

As a young Universe Denter, I tended to get very amped up as a result of what I thought was working or not working on any given project. One particularly stressful night, Michael Doyle called an abbreviated end to our work and took me out to shoot some pool, eat some protein, and turn in early. When I expressed my anxiety about how many loose ends still existed for the next day's planning workshop, Michael told me, "Being a change agent is a tough job. Our number one responsibility is to sustain our capacity to do this work over time." We made a commitment that night to take great care of ourselves first and then attend to our clients' needs.

The final two PRIMES revealed in this chapter are required gear for anyone who chooses to take a stand against the status quo. The first makes a vital distinction between being committed to verses being attached to an outcome. The other reveals how to remain in control of your way of being and how you feel, regardless of what is happening around you.

Think of these final two PRIMES as a full metal jacket for Universe Denters. Mastering them will allow you to participate in the most senior conversations on the planet in some of the most complicated and vexing circumstances while maintaining balance, curiosity, and an appreciation for the moment you are experiencing.

Traveling is brutality. It forces you to trust strangers and to lose sight of all that familiar comfort of home and friends. You are constantly off balance. Nothing is yours except the essential things — air, sleep, reams, the sea, the sky — all things tending towards the eternal or what we imagine of it.

ॐ Cesare Pavese[1]

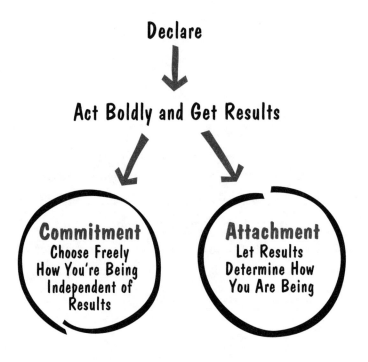

COMMITMENT VERSUS **ATTACHMENT**

COMMITMENT versus ATTACHMENT

Why saying "This project makes me so frustrated" is irrational.

Your highest priority is to take great care of yourself so that you can persist. Change agents have to be stronger than the status quo and healthier than the rest of the world.

The COMMITMENT versus ATTACHMENT PRIME will serve you as much personally as it will in your role as someone who takes a stand for new possibilities. This PRIME revealed itself to me in the strangest place:

> In the summer of 2008, my daughter Carli invited me to come along with her friends and my niece Katie on a road trip to Ohio to attend the Jerry Garcia Gathering. After 10 hours spent muscling an RV along I-70, we arrived at the gate. A woman named Anna greeted us, took our tickets, and told us where to park. She was in her fifties, with clear blue eyes; she had long, straight, red hair parted in the middle; and she wore a bright, flowing sundress. Anna looked like everything that was right about the 1960s.

> I pulled the camper into a huge and nearly empty venue that had the capacity to accommodate 100,000 people. However, this festival drew only about 200 paid attendees. It felt like the musicians and vendors outnumbered the crowd. On the second morning, I decided to give the kids some space. I sat with Anna at the gate. A few dozen people trickled in over the course of an hour or so.

I learned that Anna was a mother of four and a teacher in one of the local schools. Her family was involved in promoting the event. I asked her how she could be so peaceful and relaxed in light of the fact that hardly anyone had shown up and she and her family were going to lose some real money.

Anna explained that her family was committed to the event and had done what they could to make it available to as many people as possible. Now she was content to take what came. She had made a choice in her life to be content regardless of how the world showed up. She said, "We committed to the outcome, but we never attached to it."

From that moment, I had a special time. I introduced Anna and her family to my niece, my daughter, and her friends, and we ended up tie-dying t-shirts with the words "Not Attached to the Outcome" emblazoned across the back. I still wear mine with pride and fond memories.

Anna and her family were up to something big and meaningful and had distinguished COMMITMENT from ATTACHMENT. Because they were committed, they did everything they could to produce a wonderful music festival, then took what they got. Anna's demeanor and sense of being was the result of her free choice, as opposed to letting the outcome determine her happiness.

Suppose you and your group make a DECLARATION with INTEGRITY. Regardless of whether you are COMMITTED or ATTACHED, you live unreasonably and do everything in your power to realize the declared outcome on time. The difference between COMMITMENT and ATTACHMENT only shows up in how you let the actual outcome influence how you feel and appear to others. You are attached if you become angry because you did not fulfill your DECLARATION. People who get attached to things allow those things to determine their feelings.

Solving problems, driving change, and causing transformation are fraught with variables—unexpected risks and developments that are outside your control. Getting attached to outcomes means that you relinquish control of your way of being—and you will burn out in this business. So commit to outcomes, live unreasonably, and do everything you can to deliver the outcome on time. Then take what you get and choose freely how you want to feel and appear to others.

If thou art pained by any external thing, it is not this that disturbs thee, but thy own judgment about it. And it is in thy power to wipe out this judgment now.

❧ Marcus Aurelius

Be
Notice
Choose
Be

BE

BE

How good are you at cutting grass when you are cutting grass?

The BE PRIME reveals a simple way to give yourself the freedom to BE how you want to BE, independent from everything that is going on around you. This is essential if you are going to cause transformation because by their very nature, the activities required to do so cause turbulence and resistance, and can even compel people to act out against you. Outfitting yourself with the BE PRIME will enable you to play full out in any realm you choose while keeping control of your emotions and sense of being.

I discovered the BE PRIME while working with a group from the Women Presidents' Organization (WPO). This group gives women who are leading companies a place to exchange insights with their contemporaries, learn together, and support each other. This particular meeting took place at the height of the global financial meltdown in 2010. These leaders had been guiding their organizations through the crisis for several years. The challenges were beginning to take their toll.

These leaders understood the COMMITMENT VERSUS ATTACHMENT PRIME. We were looking for a way to master the discipline required to be powerful leaders yet remain unattached to the chaos and day-to-day stresses. One of the participants helped us realize a critical element to controlling our "way of being" and not letting our circumstances control it—and this was to "notice" our way of being. She and the others eventually stripped the essence of "controlling your way of being regardless of your circumstances" down to four steps:

1. **BE**: Acknowledge that at any point in time, you are being some way.

2. **NOTICE**: Regularly pause what you are doing and *notice* how you are being.

3.   **CHOOSE**: In that moment of noticing, choose any way of being.

4.   **BE**: Instantly become that chosen way of being.

The BE PRIME makes it possible for you to be in the midst of a huge issue with everybody screaming and acting out. The clock is ticking, and the group is getting nowhere. You take a second while all this is going on to notice that you have been drawn into the chaos by becoming frustrated and even angry. You have a sense of resentment toward one or two of the others in the room. You cannot remember choosing to be this way. It just happened.

In that second, you choose peaceful and powerful as your way of being. Nothing in your circumstances has changed. The room is still filled with hostility. You then intervene with the group from a place of peacefulness and power. And people take notice.

The BE PRIME is not about one way of being over another. It has nothing to do with how you are *supposed* to be. That is all up to you. It simply reveals how you can be any way you want to be, regardless of what is happening around you. That is it. Be angry if you want. Be happy. Be courageous. Be loving. Be mad. Be assertive. Be tranquil. Be charismatic. Be reverent. Be skeptical. Be any way you choose to be. Just be it because you choose to be it—not because the situation caused you. When outfitted with the BE PRIME, you and you alone are forever the source of how you are being and how you are showing up to others.

The PRIMES collectively have revealed much to me as I stand for bringing new possibilities forward in this world. The BE PRIME is the one I cherish most. Outfitted with BE, I am the source of my way of being, regardless of circumstance.

That afternoon in Miami, the WPO members and I went on to develop a way to discipline ourselves regarding taking full responsibility for our way of being. We imagined putting four shiny pebbles in our pockets each morning. Each time we took the time to BE–NOTICE–CHOOSE–BE, we would move a pebble from one pocket to the other. Our initial goal was to move all four pebbles during the course of the first week. The second week, we set our goal as moving the four pebbles each day. The third week, we made it our goal to move the four pebbles once in the morning and once in the afternoon. By the third week, a habit was formed—one I strongly encourage you to adopt yourself.

CONCLUSION

NOW WHAT?

Now what? That is easy. Outfit yourself with a few of the PRIMES, run out onto the court of life, and make your dent!

Life should NOT be a journey to the grave with the intention of arriving safely in an attractive and well preserved body, But rather to skid in sideways, chocolate in one hand, wine in the other, body thoroughly used up, totally worn out and screaming "WOO HOO what a ride!"

❧ Anonymous

If, along the way, you have questions or could use some support, I invite you to reach out to us at www.theprimes.com.

If you want to tackle truly wicked, socially complex, high stakes problems, you may want to connect with the folks at The Clearing consultancy. This group of passionate, highly skilled experts, are outfitting change agents like you with all the PRIMES—focusing on POWER, CORE PRIME, and REDPOINT—to help clear the critical path so you and your organization can play full out. I invite you to contact these Universe Denters at www.theclearing.com.

My request is that you let me know what you are up to and how the PRIMES are occurring to you. Please tell me about your favorite PRIME. Also, if you discover a PRIME or have suggestions about how we can better present these PRIMES, please let us know. Live Huge!

—**Chris McGoff**

NOTES

INTRODUCTION

1. Marianne Williamson, "Our Deepest Fear," *A Return to Love: Reflections on the Principles of a Course in Miracles*.

PART I: UNIVERSAL PATTERNS FOR LEADING IN UNCERTAIN TIMES

1. Ralph Waldo Emerson (May 25, 1803–April 27, 1882) was an American lecturer, philosopher, essayist, and poet best remembered for leading the Transcendentalist movement of the mid-nineteenth century. He was seen as a champion of individualism and a prescient critic of the countervailing pressures of society. He disseminated his thoughts through dozens of published essays and more than 1,500 public lectures across the United States.

CHAPTER 1

1. Hesiod (ca. 750–650 BC) was a major source of Greek mythology. He is also credited with contributions to economics, astronomy, and farming techniques.

2. David Campbell is the founder of Saks Fifth Avenue.

3. For more on the idea of IN–ON, see Michael Gerber's book *The E-Myth Revisited*, ISBN 0-88730-728-0.

4. Russell L. Ackoff, *Creating the Corporate Future* (New York: John Wiley & Sons, 1981). Dr. Ackoff looks deeply into the study of transformation. He calls those who engage in this type of planning "interactivists." They ascribe to the belief that "the future is largely subject to creation." Dr. Ackoff primarily focuses on system-level transformation. On an individual level, the concept of transformation has also been proffered by many writers within the self-help and human potential movement, most

notably by Carl Rogers, Alan Watts, Fernando Flores, Abraham Maslow, Werner Erhart, Victor Frankl, and Alexander Everett.

5. Activity-Based Costing, Six Sigma, Balanced Score Card, and Economic Value Add are just a few of the current methodologies that begin with a decomposition of the systems and processes and then attach a metric to selected parts in an effort to improve performance. Each method has value limited to "making what you have better, faster, and cheaper." These methods are less useful when what you are seeking is something new.

6. Abraham Lincoln (1809–1865) was the 16th president of the United States.

CHAPTER 2

1. Matthew 5:37. The words of Jesus Christ as recorded in the first Gospel, authored by Matthew of Galilee (37 AD).

2. Zig Ziglar (Hilary Hinton "Zig" Ziglar, 1926–) is an American author, salesperson, and motivational speaker. He has published more than 48 works, including the 2007 book *God's Way Is Still the Best Way*.

3. W. H. Murray (March 18, 1913–March 19, 1996) was a Scottish mountaineer and writer, one of a group of active mountain climbers, mainly from Clydeside, before and just after World War II. He wrote *The Scottish Himalayan Expedition* (1951).

4. Dennis Whittle and his team at Global Giving are building an efficient, open, thriving marketplace that connects people who have community and world-changing ideas with people who can support them. See www.globalgiving.org.

5. Yoda was the Jedi Master in *Star Wars*.

6. For more information about DECLARATION, I encourage you to read John R. Searle's book *Speech Acts* (Cambridge University Press, 1969). This book gives excellent treatment to the idea that words do not simply lead to action. Rather, words, spoken with integrity, are literally the action itself.

7. John Quincy Adams (July 11, 1767–February 23, 1848) was the sixth president of the United States from 1825 to 1829. He was also an American diplomat and served in both the Senate and House of Representatives.

CHAPTER 3

1. Plato (428/427 BC–348/347 BC) was a classical Greek philosopher, mathematician, student of Socrates, writer of philosophical dialogues, and founder of the Academy in Athens, the first institution of higher learning in the Western world. Along with his mentor, Socrates, and his student, Aristotle, Plato helped to lay the foundations of Western philosophy and science.

2. Patanjali (150 BC or 2nd c. BC) compiled the Yoga Sūtras to codify the practice of yoga.

3. The story of the priest came from James MacGregor Burns, who wrote *Transforming Leadership* (New York: Grove Press, 2003). This book presents case studies of leaders who took up the mantle to lead large-scale transformation activities. Burns explores the difference between change and transformation in the second chapter, which he opens with the statement, "Of all the tasks on the work agenda of leadership analysis, first and foremost is an understanding of human change, because its nature is the key to the rest."

4. John Muir (April 21, 1838–December 24, 1914) was a Scottish-born American naturalist, author, and early advocate of preservation of wilderness in the United States. His activism helped save Yosemite Valley, Sequoia National Park, and other wilderness areas. The Sierra Club, which he founded, is now one of the most important conservation organizations in the United States.

PART 2: UNIVERSAL PATTERNS OF POWERFUL ALLIANCES

1. Michael, Krigsman, *Study: 68 percent of IT projects fail*, ZDNet.com (2008).

2. Albert Einstein (March 14, 1879–April 18, 1955) was a German-born theoretical physicist who discovered the theory of general relativity, effecting a revolution in physics. For this achievement, Einstein is often regarded as the father of modern physics.

CHAPTER 4

1. Rufus E. Miles, "Miles' Law," *Public Administration Review* (© 1978) American Society for Public Administration.

2. G. K. Chesterton (May 29, 1874–June 14, 1936) was an English writer. His prolific and diverse output included philosophy, ontology, poetry, play writing, journalism, public lecturing and debating, literary and art criticism, biography, Christian apologetics, and fiction, including fantasy and detective fiction.

3. Peter McWilliams (August 5, 1949–June 14, 2000) was a writer and self-publisher of best-selling self-help books. He was an advocate for those suffering from depression. In his later years, he was a cannabis activist.

4. For more information on S-curves, see Everett M. Rogers, *Diffusion of Innovation* (New York: Free Press, 1962). Rogers first introduced the "Innovation Adoption Curve" in 1962 as a way to explain how corn farmers in Iowa adopted or resisted new technologies. He quantified laggards as about 16 percent of any given system. In 1991, Geoffrey Moore used the same idea in his book *Crossing the Chasm* (New York: HarperCollins, 1991, 1999, 2002). Moore illustrated how high-tech innovations were being adopted by the markets during the Internet expansion. Both authors provide relevant insights for today's Universe Denters.

5. Peter DiGiammarino is a Washington, DC–based management consultant. See www.intelliven.com.

CHAPTER 5

1. Peter Senge is the author of *The Fifth Discipline* and Director of the Center for Organizational Learning at the MIT Sloan School of Management.

2. T. S. Eliot (September 26, 1888–January 4, 1965), an American-born English poet, playwright, and literary critic, is arguably the most important English-language poet of the twentieth century. The poem that made his name, *The Love Song of J. Alfred Prufrock*—started in 1910 and published in Chicago in 1915—is regarded as a masterpiece of the modernist movement. He followed this with what have become some of the best-known poems in the English language, including *Gerontion* (1920), *The Waste Land* (1922), *The Hollow Men* (1925), *Ash Wednesday* (1930), and *Four Quartets* (1945). He is also known for his seven plays, particularly *Murder in the Cathedral* (1935). He was awarded the Nobel Prize in Literature in 1948.

3. Gregory Bateson (May 9, 1904–July 4, 1980) was a British anthropologist, social scientist, linguist, visual anthropologist, semiotician, and cyberneticist whose work intersected that of many other fields.

Some of his most noted writings are to be found in his books *Steps to an Ecology of Mind* (1972) and *Mind and Nature* (1979).

4. Martin Luther (November 10, 1483–February 18, 1546) was a German priest and professor of theology who initiated the Protestant Reformation. He strongly disputed the claim that freedom from God's punishment of sin could be purchased with money. He confronted indulgence salesman Johann Tetzel with his *95 Theses* in 1517.

5. W. C. Stone (May 4, 1902–September 3, 2002) was a businessman, philanthropist, and self-help book author.

CHAPTER 6

1. Wilfred Peterson (August 21, 1900–June 2, 1995) was born in Whitehall, Michigan, and lived most of his life in Grand Rapids, where he was the Vice President and Creative Director of an advertising firm, the Jaqua Company. He was regarded as "one of the best loved American writers of the twentieth century, renowned for his inspirational wisdom and aphoristic wit" by the Independent Publishers Group. He was a frequent contributor to *This Week* magazine, *Science of Mind* magazine, and *Readers Digest*.

2. Responses to Subcommittee Post-Hearing Questions Regarding the FBI's Management Practices and Acquisition of a New Investigative Case Management System GAO-06-302R (Dec 21, 2005).

3. KPMG, *Mergers and Acquisitions: Global Research Report* (2009).

4. *Meditations* (Τὰ εἰς ἑαυτόν, Ta eis heauton, literally "thoughts/writings addressed to himself") is a series of personal writings by Marcus Aurelius, Roman Emperor, 161–180 AD, in which he sets forth his ideas on Stoic philosophy.

5. Mark Jenkins (b. 1970 in Fairfax, Virginia) is an American artist most widely known for the street installations he creates using box sealing tape. His work has been featured in various publications, including *Time*, *The Washington Post*, Reuters, and *The Independent* and on the street art blog Wooster Collective. He has exhibited his work in major cities, including New York, Moscow, London, and Tokyo. He currently lives in Washington, DC.

PART 3: UNIVERSAL PATTERNS OF OUTSTANDING GROUP PERFORMANCE

CHAPTER 7

1. Brian Koslow is a manager at Rodabi Demographic Info. in the Miami–Fort Lauderdale area.

2. Herbert Bayard Swope (January 5, 1882—June 20, 1958) was a US editor and journalist. Born in St. Louis, Missouri, he was the younger brother of businessman Gerard Swope. Swope spent most of his career at the *New York World* newspaper. He was the first recipient of the Pulitzer Prize for Reporting in 1917 for a series of articles titled "Inside the German Empire." The articles formed the basis of the 1917 book *Inside the German Empire: In the Third Year of the War*, which he wrote with James W. Gerard.

3. Michael Doyle and David Straus, *How to Make Meetings Work*, Copyright © 1976, ISBN 0-515-09048-4.

CHAPTER 8

1. Ayn Rand, born Alisa Zinov'yevna Rosenbaum (February 2 [O.S. January 20], 1905–March 6, 1982), was a Russian-American novelist, philosopher, playwright, and screenwriter. She is known for her two best-selling novels and for developing a philosophical system she called Objectivism. Born and educated in Russia, Rand migrated to the United States in 1926. She worked as a screenwriter in Hollywood and had a play produced on Broadway in 1935–1936. She first achieved fame with her 1943 novel, *The Fountainhead*. Over a decade later, she published her magnum opus, the philosophical novel *Atlas Shrugged*, in 1957.

2. Larry Danner is the headmaster at Washington Christian Academy and an education consultant.

CHAPTER 9

1. Fernando Flores. I first met Fernando when we were both designing groupware in the early days of network-based personal computers. He had founded Action Technologies, a software company, where he introduced new distinctions in workflow analysis, groupware, software design, and business process analysis, which he developed in association with Terry Winograd. The basis of this application was the distinction of Request. I encourage you to read the book he coauthored with Robert Solomon,

Building Trust: In Business, Politics, Relationships, and Life (ISBN 0-19-512685-8), for more information on action-oriented language.

2. Baltasar Gracian (January 8, 1601–December 6, 1658) was a Spanish Jesuit and Baroque prose writer. He was born in Belmonte, near Calatayud (Aragon).

CHAPTER 10

1. Andrew Lang (March 31, 1844–July 20, 1912) was a Scots poet, novelist, and literary critic and contributor to the field of anthropology. He is best known as a collector of folk and fairy tales. The Andrew Lang Lectures at the University of St. Andrews are named for him.

2. Sir Richard Steele (bap. March 12, 1672–September 1, 1729) was an Irish writer and politician who is remembered as cofounder, with his friend Joseph Addison, of the magazine *The Spectator*.

3. Niccolo Machiavelli (May 3, 1469–June 21, 1527) was an Italian philosopher, humanist, and writer based in Florence during the Renaissance. He is one of the main founders of modern political science. He was a diplomat, political philosopher, playwright, and civil servant of the Florentine Republic. He also wrote comedies, carnival songs, poetry, and some of the most well-known personal correspondence in the Italian language.

PART 4: UNIVERSAL PATTERNS OF GROUP FAILURE

1. H. G. Wells (September 21, 1866–August 13, 1946) was an English author, now best known for his work in the science fiction genre. He was also a prolific writer in many other genres, including contemporary novels, history, politics, and social commentary; he even wrote textbooks. Together with Jules Verne and Hugo Gernsback, Wells has been referred to as "The Father of Science Fiction."

CHAPTER 11

1. H. L. Mencken (September 12, 1880–January 29, 1956) was an American journalist, essayist, magazine editor, satirist, acerbic critic of American life and culture, and a student of American English. Mencken, known as the "Sage of Baltimore," is regarded as one of the most influential American writers and prose stylists of the first half of the twentieth century.

CHAPTER 12

1. Rumi (1207–1273) was a thirteenth-century Persian Muslim poet, jurist, theologian, and Sufi mystic.

2. In the section on RIGHT VERSUS RIGHT, I draw heavily on the work of Dr. Rushworth Kidder. Dr. Kidder is President and Founder of the Institute for Global Ethics and the author of *How Good People Make Tough Choices* (ISBN 0-684-81838-8) and *Moral Courage* (ISBN 0-06-059154-4). Dr. Kidder's newest book is called *Good Kids, Tough Choices* (ISBN 978-0-470-54762-5).

3. George Bernard Shaw (1856–1950) was an Irish playwright and cofounder of the London School of Economics. Although his first profitable writing was music and literary criticism, in which capacity he wrote many highly articulate pieces of journalism, his main talent was for drama; he wrote more than 60 plays. Nearly all his writings deal sternly with prevailing social problems but have a vein of comedy to make their stark themes more palatable. Shaw examined education, marriage, religion, government, health care, and class privilege.

4. W. H. Auden (1907–1973), regarded by many as one of the greatest writers and poets of the twentieth century, investigated the relationship between unique human beings and the anonymous, impersonal world of nature.

CHAPTER 13

1. Henry Ford (July 30, 1863–April 7, 1947) was a prominent American industrialist, the founder of the Ford Motor Company, and sponsor of the development of the assembly line technique of mass production.

2. Henry Miller (December 26, 1891–June 7, 1980) was an American novelist and painter. He was known for breaking with existing literary forms and developing a new sort of "novel" that is a mixture of novel, autobiography, social criticism, philosophical reflection, surrealist free association, and mysticism—one that is distinctly always about and expressive of the real-life Henry Miller and yet is also fictional.

CHAPTER 14

1. King Whitney Jr., born Whitney M. Young Jr. (July 31, 1921, Lincoln Ridge, Kentucky–March 11, 1971, Lagos, Nigeria), was an articulate US civil rights leader who spearheaded the drive for equal

opportunity for blacks in US industry and government service during his 10 years as head of the National Urban League (1961–71), the world's largest social–civil rights organization.

2. Sir Edmund Hillary (July 20, 1919–January 11, 2008) was a New Zealand mountaineer, explorer, and philanthropist. On May 29, 1953, at the age of 33, he and Sherpa mountaineer Tenzing Norgay became the first climbers known to have reached the summit of Mount Everest.

3. The Moody Blues are an English rock band. Among their innovations was a fusion with classical music, most notably in their 1967 album *Days of Future Passed*. The Moody Blues have sold in excess of 70 million albums worldwide and have been awarded 14 platinum and gold discs. As of 2011, they remain active, with one member from the original band from 1964 and two from the 1967 lineup.

PART 5: UNIVERSAL PATTERNS OF THRIVING IN AMBIGUITY

CHAPTER 15

1. Plutarch of Chaeronea in Boeotia (ca. 45–120 AD) was a Platonist philosopher best known as the author of *Parallel Lives*, which paired Greek and Roman statesmen and military leaders. He was a prolific writer who also authored a collection of *moralia*, or ethical essays, mostly in dialogue format, many of them devoted to philosophical topics and not at all limited to ethics.

2. Nielsen, The Mobile Media Report: State of the Media Q3 2011.

3. Iqbal, Shamsi and Eric Horvitz. "Disruption and Recovery of Computing Tasks: Field Study, Analysis, and Direction" (2007).

4. Jean de la Fontaine (July 8, 1621, Château-Thierry–April 13, 1695, Paris) was the most famous French fabulist and one of the most widely read French poets of the seventeenth century.

5. Beatrice Bruteau is an American philosopher and author best known for her work in spiritual evolution.

CHAPTER 16

1. Cesare Pavese (1908–1950) was an Italian poet, novelist, literary critic, and translator. He is widely considered to be among the major authors of the twentieth century in his home country.

INDEX OF THE PRIMES

(alphabetical)

PRIME	PAGE
A CLEARING	209
BE	223
BIG HAT—LITTLE HAT	171
BLIND MEN AND THE ELEPHANT	51
BREACH	137
CHANGE VERSUS TRANSFORMATION	13
CHASE—LOSE	183
COHESION	83
COMMITMENT VERSUS ATTACHMENT	219
CONFUSION	203
CONGRUENCE	119
CONSENSUS	105
CORE PRIME	65
COURT—LOCKER ROOM	199
CULTURE	115
DECLARATION	29
DYNAMIC INCOMPLETENESS	35
ENNOBLEMENT	39
FACTS, STORIES, AND BELIEFS	147
FEEDBACK AS CARING	123
FRAGMENTATION	161
GOSSIP	151

IN–ON 9

INTEGRITY 21

ISSUES FORWARD 213

LAGGARDS 157

LEADERSHIP SPECTRUM 101

LEADING 5

LEVELS OF PERSPECTIVE 55

MUDA 93

OPEN–CLOSE–DECIDE 109

PARITY 73

PERIMETER 143

POWER 45

PROCESS–CONTENT 189

REDPOINT 85

REQUEST 129

RESOLUTION PRINCIPLES 179

RIGHT VERSUS RIGHT 175

SAME–DIFFERENT 165

S-CURVES 59

SHAPE SHIFTING 191

STAKE 77

TRUST THE UNIVERSE 25

TRUST 133

VICTIM–LEADER 197

ABOUT THE AUTHOR

Chris McGoff is a business builder and international consultant with over 30 years of experience as a strategic planner, problem solver, and change agent. He advises leaders of organizations and coalitions on how to drive outcomes in uncertain times.

His focus is on product and process innovation, growth strategies and vision, complex problem solving, fast track implementation, high performance groups and organizations, and value chain and customer engagement.

He is the founder of The Clearing, Inc., a strategic management consultancy headquartered in Washington, DC, that outfits organizations and coalitions with the PRIMES to enable them to tackle their most complex, high stakes problems.

A few of his larger clients include Boeing, Consol Energy, AARP, The World Bank Group, DuPont, The United Nations, IBM, Departments of Defense, Energy, State, USAID, Homeland Security, NASA, along with various state and local government. Chris McGoff is passionate about serving the needs of small and medium-sized enterprises, including those located in developing nations.

Chris is an adjunct professor at the University of Maryland's Graduate School of Public Policy, lecturing on topics related to information and technology including privacy, piracy, cyber security, cloud computing, nanotechnology, and the digital divide.

Chris McGoff is an author and a popular public speaker, currently on the subjects of "Leading Powerfully in Uncertain Times" and "Building Intentional Cultures."

Past roles include Founder of Touchstone Consulting, which he sold to SRA Corporation, and IBM where he pioneered the development of group decision support systems. He serves on various boards, including LiveWell Clinics, Nairobi, Kenya and GlobalGiving in Washington, DC.

Chris McGoff and his wife, Claire, live in the Washington, DC, area with their six children.

Now Chris shares 46 bite-sized chunks of solid wisdom and proven expertise—*The PRIMES*. His book illuminates the way forward for twenty-first century problem solvers and Universe Denters. For more information about Chris and how to apply the PRIMES, visit www.theprimes.com.

Chris McGoff (right) and Michael Doyle (left)